Difficult Questions

Difficult
Questions
in Polish-Jewish Dialogue

How Poles and Jews
See Each Other:
A Dialogue on Key Issues
in Polish-Jewish Relations

Jacek Santorski & Co Agencja Wydawnicza
Forum for Dialogue Among Nations
American Jewish Committee

English translation by Erica Lehrer
Graphic design by Maciej Szymanowicz
Cover photo by Adam Chelstowski/Forum

The book was published as part of the project carried out by the Forum for Dialogue Among Nations and the American Jewish Committee, with financial assistance from the Task Force for International Cooperation on Holocaust, Remembrance, and Research, and the Taube Foundation for Jewish Life and Culture.

First published in 2006 by Jacek Santorski & Co Agencja Wydawnicza

Printed in Poland

ISBN 978-83-89763-95-2

Jacek Santorski & Co Agencja Wydawnicza sp. z o.o.
Alzacka 15A, 03 -972 Warszawa

www.jsantorski.pl; e-mail: wydawnictwo@jsantorski.pl
trade dept.: +48 22 616 29 44, 616 29 36
fax +48 22 433 51 51

CONTENTS

TODAY

MEMORY AND KNOWLEDGE ABOUT THE HOLOCAUST

Editor's note

Over the past fifteen years the number of Jewish youth groups traveling to Poland has increased dramatically. Guests from Israel, the United States, Europe, Canada, Australia, and Latin America visit the former concentration camps in Auschwitz, Treblinka, and Belzec. They explore the remnants of the Jewish quarter in Warsaw and Cracow's Kazimierz, discover the Jewish resistance movement at the Monument to the Heroes of the Ghetto and the cemetery at Gesia, and learn about the history of the prewar Polish Jewish community. Typically, such a visit is the only opportunity these young Jews have to experience today's Poland and meet its inhabitants. For young Poles, encountering their Jewish peers is very significant. In a country where Jewish culture once blossomed, there remain today only memories—not always favorable and often stereotypical.

Meetings of young Poles and Jews organized for the past ten years in schools in Warsaw and Cracow by the Forum for Dialogue Among Nations have a unique character: They are the only opportunity for these young people to discover for themselves something of the people about whom their parents and grandparents often spoke. Research carried out in 2004 revealed that even after a brief, hour-long meeting, young Poles were significantly more likely to say that they like Jews and that they see how much, in the end, they are similar to "us." After meeting with Poles, young Jews, who often come to Poland with great trepidation, stop believing that anti-Semitism governs the world and that Jews are universally hated. Such meetings allow these young Jews to see that young Poles who are so similar to them are—as a rule—very pleasantly disposed toward Jewish visitors.

Sometimes, however, in the course of these meetings, misunderstandings occur and dialogue becomes difficult. This typically happens when the conversation turns to particularly sensitive themes: the Holocaust, the attitude of Poles during World War II, the current Middle East conflict. We set out to identify which themes present the greatest difficulty for dialogue among young Poles and Jews. But we realized the difficulty these young people had in even formulating many of the "difficult questions" they would have liked answered; they worried that even putting them into words might offend the "other side." When such questions did arise in the course of a Polish-Jewish encounter, the result was open contention—some people became agitated, others burst into tears.

We decided to ask young Poles and Jews to write down their "difficult questions"—the most sensitive ones they could think of. In Polish, American, and Israeli schools, as well as among groups visiting Poland from Israel, the United States, Canada, and Australia, we handed out a total of 1,065 questionnaires for young Poles and Jews to tell us, without inhibition, which questions relating to Poles and Jews seem to them the hardest to confront.

A group of sociologists connected to the Forum for Dialogue Among Nations analyzed the resulting questionnaires and selected those questions that appeared most frequently, and those issues that young people judged to be the most relevant.

At the same time, our sociologists made their own observations during meetings in schools, during the March of the Living in Auschwitz, and at the Warsaw Ghetto. Thus, they supplemented their findings from organized meetings with direct observations about what provoked the most controversy under "natural" conditions. The goal was to uncover the questions that most inhibit dialogue between Poles and Jews.

We compiled a list of fifty questions for publication, and asked experts in the fields of history, sociology, Polish-Jewish relations, and religion to answer the questions posed by young Poles and Jews. The result of their work is the book you are holding in your hands. We hope that it will foster mutual understanding and learning and help to abolish stereotypes, myths, and misunderstandings. It will also be a valuable resource for the educational workshops and Polish-Jewish youth dialogue programs organized by the Forum for Dialogue Among Nations.

For clarity the questions are color-differentiated. Blue are the questions posed by Jewish youth, red are the questions posed by young Poles.

Finally, we would like to thank Wladyslaw Bartoszewski, Guy Billauer, Stanislaw Krajewski, Jan Jagielski, Helena Datner and Robert

Szuchta for content consulting, research organization, and selection of the final list of questions. We would also like to thank a group of sociologists who carried out the research on Difficult Questions in Polish-Jewish Dialogue: Adam Ostolski, Adrian Wojcik and Aleksandra Wysocka. Finally, we offer our heartfelt thanks to Polish schools and groups of Jewish youth who took part in the research and all the individuals and institutions who made their photographs accessible for this publication. Without the support of all these people, this book would not have been possible.

We also thank our American partner, the American Jewish Committee, for financial and content-related support of our project and in preparation of this book. And we offer particular thanks to the Task Force for International Cooperation on Holocaust Education, Remembrance and Research, the Taube Foundation for Jewish Life & Culture, and Zygmunt Rolat for financial support of our project.

Maciej Kozlowski, Andrzej Folwarczny,
and Michal Bilewicz
Difficult Questions Editorial Team

PREFACE
BY WLADYSLAW BARTOSZEWSKI

On the threshold of the twenty-first century, attempts are finally being made—late, but not too late, to fill out the picture of the interethnic, social, and political relations between Poles and Polish Jews. These attempts may lead to critical re-evaluations not only of Jewish behavior, but also of that of Poles and of Europe, and even of the entire world in the twentieth century. For obvious reasons, a central focus of this historical examination is the years when the Third Reich, led personally by Adolf Hitler and his National Socialist Party (NSDAP) and supported by a significant majority of Germans, planned for extermination of European Jewry. The phenomenon, which was ideologically and politically organized by the German state, was unique in its attempt to exterminate an entire nation—many millions of people, regardless of gender or age. Known today as the *Shoah* or Holocaust, this event absorbs the attention and captures the imagination not only of historians, but also of significant numbers of ordinary people in Europe, Israel, the United States, and elsewhere.

Although Poland was not the only site of the Nazi genocide, during the years 1941-45, the *Shoah*'s central stage was the territory of the Polish Republic under German occupation, both within its 1939 state borders and in the adjacent eastern and southeastern territories (the Baltic States, Belarus, Ukraine, and Romania). After the defeat of the Third Reich, all the nation states in that part of Europe found themselves within the orbit of the totalitarian Communist regime of Stalin and his successors, leaving them deprived of political sovereignty and basic freedoms. A half century under Soviet domination had terrible consequences for the knowledge of basic historical facts, as two generations were denied the opportunity to form independent historical consciousness free from constraint. In a society living under a mask of lies, accepting untruths or half-truths became the norm. This was the case even in the realm of basic facts, such as statistical facts, let alone in their interpretation. It was difficult for people to speak or think and, even more so, to engage in a process of societal therapy or healing of wounds. The commendable efforts made by many Polish and Jewish historians, and by witnesses to the events surrounding World War II, who felt the need to build bridges between the followers of Christianity and Judaism, and especially between Poles and Jews of varied traditions or worldviews, certainly played a meaningful role in nurturing understanding and goodwill. However, they could not do so in a truly adequate or satisfying way.

The majority of Jews and Poles living today in Poland, Israel, and the world over do not relate to the events leading up to and during World War II as do those with personal experiences or with the reflection of a participant or a witness of these events. Among elderly Jews and Poles, there is clear polarization of historical narratives, and among historians, these distinct narratives are outlined as two truths: a Jewish truth and a Polish truth. This is determined, of course, not only by differences of beliefs or family traditions, but perhaps more so, by where one happened to live after World War II. Today, Poles and Jews living in Poland, under conditions of freedom and democracy, have the right to expect answers to many apparently straightforward questions about their history. Clarifications of these historical matters should correspond to various levels of knowledge and experience, and should serve the future generations of Poles and Jews, wherever they may reside. They should aid in overcoming stereotypes on both sides, particularly concerning their self-images, tendency to surrender to half-truths, and the danger of giving way to populist simplifications.

It is clear that no publication can be a universal remedy against hatred or ill will. But dialogue—under conditions of an honest search for truth, with mutual respect, sympathy, and sensitivity, and recognition of the traumas caused during infernally difficult times—is necessary for us all. There is no other way.

In recent years, relations between the Polish Republic and the State of Israel have been at their best. Relations of Polish institutions with important Jewish Diaspora organizations in the United States and France are also increasingly positive. Convincing examples of this cooperation include the joint project of the Polish government and the American Jewish Committee in establishing a fitting memorial at the site of the former Nazi death camp at Belzec, where nearly 500,000

Jews were murdered, as well as events, and indeed the entire atmosphere, surrounding the January 2005 ceremonies commemorating the sixtieth anniversary of the liberation of the German extermination center at Auschwitz-Birkenau.

The publication of *Difficult Questions* is a helpful step on a path which we must travel in our quest toward a better future for all people of goodwill.

PROF. WLADYSLAW BARTOSZEWSKI is a historian, former Polish minister of foreign affairs, co-founder of the Polish *Zegota* Council for Aid to Jews, holder of "the Righteous Among the Nations" distinction, participant in the Warsaw Uprising of 1944, and former prisoner of KL Auschwitz. He is also the director of the International Auschwitz Council for the Polish Government, and an honorary citizen of the State of Israel.

INTRODUCTION
BY DAVID A. HARRIS

Poland and the Jewish people have been interconnected for more than one thousand years. It is simply impossible to talk of Polish history without understanding the Jewish dimension. Equally, it is impossible to talk of Jewish history without understanding the Polish dimension.

Jews formed a substantial percentage of the Polish population. On the eve of World War II, for example, fully 10 percent of Poles were Jews, and one-third of Warsaw's population was Jewish. Moreover, Jews played a vibrant role in virtually every aspect of Polish life. And, for centuries, Poland was quite literally the epicenter of world Jewry. Volumes have been written about the rich tapestry of Jewish life that evolved throughout the land.

But this millennial relationship has not been without its complications.

It has had its high—and low—points. Anyone looking to prove a particular perspective is likely to find sufficient supporting data. Thus, those who argue that the relationship has been essentially positive are able to marshal evidence underscoring the many instances of tolerance, synergy, and cooperation. And, similarly, those who insist that the link has been largely defined by difficulty and distance will find no shortage of examples to make their point.

I have been in enough meetings over the years to hear angry accusations exchanged by the two sides—from Jews who don't have a kind thing to say about Poland, and from Poles, whether they live in Poland or the United States, who have little good to say about Jews. Conversely, I have been in many settings where the bonds between the two groups could not have been stronger.

Our view at the American Jewish Committee is that the relationship is simply too important to be left to those with no interest in or ability to move it forward. Of course, an understanding of history is vital, even if at times there may be competing historical narratives and no easy way to reconcile them. But, at the same time, being students of history must never translate into becoming its prisoners. In our work, we believe profoundly in the possibility—indeed, the necessity—of seeking to write new chapters in history, based on mutual respect and mutually beneficial collaboration.

This approach certainly applies to Poland. In 1989, Poland courageously broke free from Soviet hegemony and embarked on an exciting, if challenging, new era. After suffering from more than four decades of Communist tyranny, preceded by the devastation wrought by the Nazi invasion and occupation, Poland finally had the chance to reconnect with its democratic heritage, ensure the security of its borders, and build a robust new society, closely linked to both Europe and the United States.

Also noteworthy was the eagerness with which many Poles sought contact with Israel and the Jewish people—a phenomenon witnessed throughout much of Central and Eastern Europe in the wake of Communism's defeat.

Perhaps it was a response to the Communist period, when ties with Israel had been severely curtailed and anti-Semitism was used as a convenient political tool. Perhaps it was a genuine curiosity about the deep-seated place of Jews in Polish history and culture, which had been a no-go zone for so many years. Perhaps it was a result of the discovery of Jewish roots in many Polish families. And perhaps it was a belief that the new Poland would be judged, in part at least, by how it dealt with the demons of its past.

And so, willing individuals from both sides took advantage of the post-1989 opening to reach out to one another. Prominent among them was my fellow author of an introduction to this book, Professor Wladyslaw Bartoszewski—Auschwitz survivor, distinguished former foreign minister of Poland, and cherished friend of the Jewish people.

With the passage of each year, the points of contact have both widened and deepened. This is especially noticeable in the bilateral link between Poland and Israel. In fact, the relationship has taken off in many striking directions, and leaders of the two nations today refer to one another as partners and friends. Elsewhere, progress has been more uneven, though there are certainly advances to report—many involving the efforts of the American Jewish Committee, which has devoted considerable attention to seizing the previously unimaginable opportunities made possible in the post-Communist era.

In May 2005, I published a piece calling for greater contact and mutual understanding, citing the annual March of the Living as one initiative deserving more attention. I was struck, even sixteen years into this new era, by the tenor of some of the letters I received in response—both from Jews saying they would never forgive Poles for crimes of anti-Semitism and asserting that there was nothing "new" about today's Poland, and from non-Jewish Poles insisting that Jews were responsible for the onset of Communism in Poland and made a hobby of defaming Poland. To be fair, other letters, at least as numerous, were strongly supportive of my plea.

This book, built around actual questions raised in Polish-Jewish encounters, is our way of acknowledging two central points. First, the topic of Polish-Jewish relations is immensely important—not just for considering the past, but, every bit as much, for charting the future. And second, let's be honest; there have been some tough issues. But rather than either bury them or simply talk past one another, we believe they should be thoughtfully and constructively considered, which is precisely what this book aims to do.

Do we have an ulterior motive? Yes. The American Jewish Committee and our partner, the Polish-based Forum for Dialogue Among the Nations, hope that this publication will contribute, especially among members of the younger generation, to building bridges, enhancing understanding, and underscoring points of commonality, of which, I might add, there are many.

It is our view, to borrow the words of Confucius, that "it is better to light a candle than to curse the darkness." This book, we trust, will rise to that worthy standard.

DAVID A. HARRIS is executive director of the American Jewish Committee. He earned his undergraduate degree in history from the University of Pennsylvania and pursued graduate studies in international relations at the London School of Economics, and at Oxford University. From 2000-2002, he was a visiting scholar at the Johns Hopkins University School of Advanced International Studies.

past

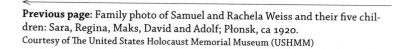

Previous page: Family photo of Samuel and Rachela Weiss and their five children: Sara, Regina, Maks, David and Adolf; Płonsk, ca 1920.
Courtesy of The United States Holocaust Memorial Museum (USHMM)

ISRAEL GUTMAN

1. Where did Jews come from to Poland and why?

The first contacts between Poles and Jews
probably took place around the time
of the establishment of the Polish state.
Given that these events are so distant, threads
of legend intertwine with actual happenings.

Crest of the village of Kolbuszowa, from 1785, presenting a friendly handshake between a Pole and a Jew.

Matzeva (tombstone) of Cantor David from 1203, the oldest preserved headstone from the territory of Poland.
Photo by T. Jankowski

The first contacts between Poles and Jews probably took place around the time of the establishment of the Polish state. Given that these events are so distant, threads of legend intertwine with actual happenings. A Jewish tradition says that the name Poland (*Polin* in Hebrew) comes from the two Hebrew words "*po*" and "*lin*," meaning "sleep here"—that is, here you will find rest until the coming of the Messiah.

The earliest contacts probably occurred through merchant expeditions to Polish lands, which took place in approximately the latter half of the tenth century. From the end of the twelfth century there were already historical artifacts attesting to a continuous Jewish presence in Poland. Coins preserved from the reign of Mieszko the Old (twelfth century) bear Hebrew inscriptions, providing evidence that Jews were involved in minting. Documents from the beginning of the thirteenth century testify to business transactions with Jews in the region of Wroclaw. From the middle of that century there are numerous reports of groups of Jews living in royal towns such as Cracow, Kalisz, Gniezno, Sandomierz, Plock, and Legnica, as well as in other towns in Silesia and Greater Poland.

Previous page: *Kalisian Statute* by Artur Szyk. The Kalisian Statute was a collection of privileges granted to Jews by Prince Boleslaw the Pious in the thirteenth century. Courtesy of the Jewish Historical Institute

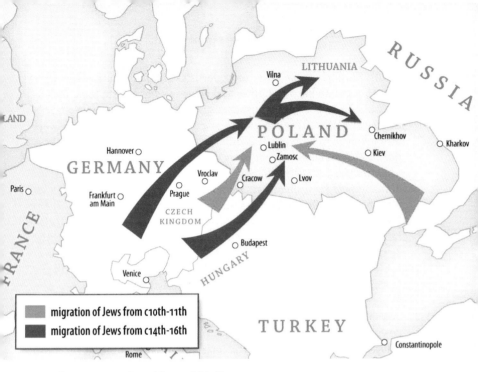

Map showing migration of Jews within Europe.

Jews came pouring into Poland from Western Europe. Documents evidence the settlement in both Poland and Hungary of Jews from Bavaria, where they were persecuted during the first Crusade. Jews settling in Poland spoke Yiddish, a dialect based on German, written in Hebrew letters. Some Jewish historians maintain that, alongside the influx of Jews from Western Europe, Jews also came to Poland from the east, relocating after the collapse in the tenth century of the Khazar state that stretched from the Caspian Sea to the Black Sea; the Khazars, under King Bulan in the eighth century, had accepted the Jewish religion, but by the tenth century had ceased to be Jewish. Advocates of this theory point to Jewish and Hebrew place names in the southeastern regions of Poland, although there is little concrete evidence to validate this hypothesis.

The reason for Jewish settlement in Poland from Western Europe was, above all, persecution. Expelled from countries in which they had lived for centuries, they found safe asylum in Poland.

Already in the early period, Jews settling in Poland formed themselves into a *kehilla*, a communal structure that facilitated the Jewish socio-religious lifestyle. A great achievement for the Jews was the creation of autonomous governing bodies in Poland, called the Council of Four

Lands. Through these structures, Jewish communal authorities were able to regulate both the inner and outer lives of Polish Jews, including taxation, resolution of disputes, and education. In this period Jews engaged in agriculture as well as trade and peddling, and at times were also involved in banking. It is difficult to estimate the number of Jews during this early period, but likely there were some few thousands.

After the destructive Mongolian invasions, Poland needed additional manpower to stimulate its economy, trade, and urbanization. Jews were not the only foreign element to be attracted; in the cities there frequently were also Germans. However, the former's position was so important that the prince of Kalisz, Boleslaw the Pious, granted the Jews broad privileges, which were further enlarged by King Kazimierz the Great. These privileges evidenced the sympathetic attitude of the leaders to the newly settling Jews. These positive relations also generally extended to the nobility. However, the bourgeoisie, to whom the Jews represented economic competition, most often expressed dislike. Jews also encountered some difficulties when it came to the Catholic Church. Columbia University historian Salo Baron, himself of Polish origin, wrote:

> In the epoch of humanism and reformation, on the periphery of the Roman Catholic world, a new Jewish center had sprung up, which in the future would fill a vital gap in the history of the Jewish nation. At a time when places of Jewish residence in Western and Central Europe were extinguishing their lamps, they were simultaneously multiplying on the Vistula, Dniester, Dnieper, and Niemen. At the end of the sixteenth century Jews from Poland and Lithuania are reaching a dominant position among all Ashkenazi Jews, which means a dominant position in the world.

To sum up, one should emphasize that the position of Jews in the Polish Republic was, overall, positive. This was also true of the Jewish contribution to the social life of the Republic. It remained true so long as Poland was a country of broad tolerance, a fatherland of many nations; changes came about with the decline of the state, but that is another story entirely.

PROF. ISRAEL GUTMAN, born in Warsaw, is a historian. He fought in the Warsaw Ghetto Uprising and was later imprisoned in Majdanek. A professor of history at the Hebrew University in Jerusalem, he is chairman of the Scientific Council of the Yad Vashem Holocaust Memorial Institute in Jerusalem. He is also the deputy chairman of the International Auschwitz Council.

JOANNA TOKARSKA-BAKIR

▶ # 2. Where does anti-Semitism in Poland come from?

The deepest and, to the present day, most powerful causes of anti-Semitism are structural in character. Thus Polish anti-Semitism is not rooted in some "natural" Polish inclination for evil nor in some "natural" Jewish tendency to be its victim. There has been, however, a grim mechanism of evolving differences between the national and religious groups. In the process, nothing contributes to elevating one's own uncertain identity as much as distinguishing it from that of foreigners—those who are different.

Banner at the entrance to the Polytechnic in Lvov, with the inscription: "A day without Jews. We demand an official ghetto," 1937.
Courtesy of the Jewish Historical Institute

Quite distinctive, Polish strands of anti-Semitism comprise three separate types:

1. The archaic, folk anti-Semitism/anti-Judaism, based on pre-Vatican II Church teachings, from which contemporary Catholicism has distanced itself and for which it does not take any responsibility;

2. The modern anti-Semitism of Polish nationalists, to a certain degree inspired by Russian propaganda on the one hand (encouraged by the Okhrana, the czarist secret police, literature of ritual murder, and conspiracy theories like the proven forgery *The Protocols of the Elders of Zion*, which inspired pogroms at the end of the nineteenth and the first decades of the twentieth century), and on the other hand, by that of the Nazis, which still exists to this day with particular vigor;

3. The so-called "new anti-Semitism," brought about by the processes of globalization and the longstanding Palestinian-Israeli conflict, in which, from time to time, resentments based on the first two trends come into play. Paradoxically, the new anti-Semitism's most toxic com-

---

Previous page: Painting from the Church of Saint Paul in Sandomierz falsely accusing Jews of ritual murder. Photo by G. Bogacz/Forum

ponent is modern individualism, which ignores the principle of moral responsibility for the first two varieties of Polish anti-Semitism.

The deepest and, to the present day, most powerful causes of anti-Semitism are structural in character. Thus Polish anti-Semitism is not rooted in some "natural" Polish inclination for evil nor in some "natural" Jewish tendency to be its victim. There has been, however, a grim mechanism of evolving differences between the national and religious groups. In the process, nothing contributes to elevating one's own uncertain identity as much as distinguishing it from that of foreigners—those who are different.

Poland, from its early days in the "First Republic" (before 1795), has always been a multiethnic and multireligious community, which led to a tendency to imitate Jewish identity *per negationem*—defining itself by what it is not. (For example, in Hanna Krall's latest novel, *Krol kier znowu na wylocie* [The King of Hearts Is Out Again], Warsaw 2006, she describes many ways of doing things in a "Jewish way"—you can pray in this way, you can put your purse on the table in this way.)

One must also take into consideration the archaic individualism of the Poles, a trait called *warcholstwo* (quarrelsomeness), present from premodern times. This individualism was summed up in the dictum of Hasidic sage Menakhem Mendel of Kotzk: "If I am I because I am I, and you are you because you are you, then I am I and you are you. But if I am I because you are you, and you are you because I am I, then I am not I, and you are not you."

The late Middle Ages and early Renaissance were times when, through the activities of missionary orders, the spiritual journeys of figures like Priest Piotr Skarga, and the circulation of theological literature and religious art, Poland entered the mainstream of European culture. This process, hastened and strengthened by the invention of printing, led to the importation of anti-Jewish and anti-Semitic views into Poland.

Priest Przeclaw Mojecki's 1589 book, *Jewish Cruelty, Murder, and Superstitions*, rightly described by Rabbi Joshua Trachtenberg as one of the most important books in the history of Polish anti-Semitism, includes a detailed anti-Jewish theological bibliography. The book was developed during centuries of intense battles against Judaism in Western Europe—that is, England, France, the German lands, and

Spain—which by the sixteenth century had managed to completely rid themselves of their Jewish populations.

The more the Jew was demonized, the better the Pole felt about himself as a human being, a Christian, and a European—which meant primarily a "non-Jew." Only under the influence of modern post-Enlightenment conceptions of human rights, and confronted with the tragedy of the Holocaust, did Poles encounter other concepts of what it means to be a person. The problem is that, cut off by Communism from the mainstream of European life for four decades, Poland came belatedly to this understanding.

PROF. JOANNA TOKARSKA-BAKIR, a cultural anthropologist, is a lecturer at the Institute for Social Sciences at Warsaw University and head of the Department of Cultural Anthropology at Collegium Civitas. She is author of such books as: *Wyzwolenie przez zmysły. Tybetańskie idee soteriologiczne* (Liberation Through Senses: Soteriological Ideas in Tibet), 1998, *Obraz osobliwy. Hermeneutyczna lektura źródeł etnograficznych* (A Peculiar Picture: Hermeneutical Reception of Ethnographic Sources), 2000, and *Rzeczy mgliste* (Misty Objects), 2004.

JERZY TOMASZEWSKI

▸ 3. Were there pogroms in Poland?

The term "pogrom" is often used for any attack by a crowd on a national or religious minority. Pogroms in this sense occurred rarely on Polish soil; more often there were smaller-scale attacks, often resulting in the destruction of property, and the beating of a certain number of people, but rarely murder.

Children looking into a Jewish house destroyed during the anti-Jewish riots of April 1935 in Stanislawow (today Iwano-Frankowsk, Ukraine).
Courtesy of the Archives of Audio-Visual Records

Unfortunately, there were.

This term, however, has many meanings. According to the *Encyclopaedia Judaica*, "Pogrom is a Russian word designating an attack, accompanied by destruction, the looting of property, murder, and rape, perpetrated by one section of the population against another. [...] However, as an international term, the word 'pogrom' is employed in many languages to describe specifically attacks accompanied by looting and bloodshed against the Jews in Russia." The *Universal Encyclopedia PWN*, the largest Polish encyclopedia, offers the following definition: "a groupled and organized attack on a religious or national minority with the intention of intimidation, expulsion, or slaughter." The term "pogrom" is often used for any attack by a crowd on a national or religious minority.

Pogroms in this sense occurred rarely on Polish soil; more often there were smaller-scale attacks, often resulting in the destruction of property, and the beating of a certain number of people, but rarely murder.

On December 25, 1881, in Warsaw, a crowd began robbing and destroying shops, chiefly Jewish ones, initially with no response from the Russian police. On December 27, the pogrom was put in check by army troops. Nearly 2,000 Jewish and eighty Christian families suffered material damages. Rumors of Russian provocation circulated. On May 1,

←

Previous page: Anti-Jewish riots on June 6, 1936, in Minsk Mazowiecki, where shops and houses belonging to Jewish city dwellers were destroyed.
Courtesy of the Archives of Audio-Visual Records

1892, in Lodz, a workers' protest took place, with the army moving in against it. The workers were beaten and wounded. The altercation lasted a week, and near the end, there were attacks on Jewish shops and pubs. Attacks on Jewish shops also occurred on September 11, 1892, in Czestochowa, and in August 1904 in Ostrowiec Swietokrzyski. Pogroms in Bialystok in June 1905 and August 1906 were primarily committed by Russian soldiers and railwaymen.

The collapse of the German and Austrian administrations in the fall of 1918, and the subsequent wars suffered by the young Polish nation, encouraged robbery and attacks, not only on Jews. Widespread accusations of collaboration with the enemy resulted in executions of Jews. On April 5, 1919, a garrison commander in Pinsk sentenced thirty Jews, without trial, to execution by shooting. In Plock, on August 19, 1920, the wartime court sentenced a rabbi to death.

A tragic pogrom broke out in Lvov on November 22, 1918. It was influenced by a rumor that Jews had supported the Ukrainians when Polish troops drove out the Ukrainian army. Approximately fifty Jews were killed, thirty-eight houses were burned down; the crowd robbed stores, workshops, and apartments. The peasant rebellion in the Rzeszow region in the spring of 1919 had a broad social base, directed against farmers, Jews (especially traders), and the administration—admitted exploiters. After a few days, the army restored peace. Few were

Shop destroyed by a firecracker during anti-Jewish riots in Stanislawow (today Iwano-Frankowsk, Ukraine) in April 1935. Courtesy of the Archives of Audio-Visual Records

mortally wounded (among the aggressors as well), but there was great material loss. The subsequent stabilization of the Polish state resulted in a diminution in the number of pogroms in the years immediately following.

The incidents of the second half of the 1930s, when the National Democrats wielded anti-Semitism as a weapon in the fight against the government, had a different character; an economic crisis enhanced its efficacy. The nationalists propagated a boycott against Jews, and in this atmosphere, disputes in the marketplaces in many towns (often provoked by thugs) led to attacks by the crowd on stores, workshops, and less frequently on Jewish apartments. Provocative gossip circulated (in Busko in May of 1937, for example, it was said that some Jew threw a stone at a procession). The most destructive attacks occurred in the years 1935 to 1937. The largest incidents (also defined as pogroms) were in Sokoly (August 25, 1935), Odrzywole (November 20 and 27, 1935), Rawa Mazowiecka (November 28, 1935), Czyzew (December 15, 1935 and January 7, 1937), Truskolasy (January 26, 1936), Zagorow (February 5, 1936), Myslenice (the attack by thugs of the National Party on June 23, 1936), Dlugosiodlo (August 15, 1936), Zambrow (October 27, 1936), and Sniadowa (October 29, 1936).

A tragic incident took place in Odrzywole on November 29, 1935. Police bullets killed eighteen peasants; perhaps for this reason police action to protect Jews was subsequently less determined. In a few instances, incitement by the crowd led to a Jew killing a Pole. In Grodno, a murder on June 4 was followed by a pogrom on June 7, 1935; two Jews died, others were injured. In Przytyk, on March 9, 1936, two died; Jews were beaten to death and many others injured. In Minsk Mazowiecki, on June 1-4, 1936, a Jew was murdered, another few dozen wounded or beaten up, and ten houses containing eight Jews were burned down. In Brzesc, on May 13, 1937, several Jews were injured and beaten. Likewise, in Czestochowa on June 19, 1937, several were also injured and beaten, and similar events occurred on November 17 of that year in Bielsko-Biala.

PROF. JERZY TOMASZEWSKI is a historian and member of the Scientific Council of the Jewish Historical Institute. He is the author of many books on Jewish history in Poland, such as *Zarys dziejów Żydów w Polsce w latach 1918–1939* (A Short History of Jews in Poland 1918–1939), 1990, *Mniejszości narodowe w Polsce XX wieku* (National Minorities in Twentieth-Century Poland), 1991, *Preludium zagłady. Wygnanie Żydów polskich z Niemiec w 1938 r.* (A Prelude to the Shoah: Expulsion of Polish Jews from Germany in 1938), 1998.

ISRAEL GUTMAN

▶ 4. How many Jews actually died during the Holocaust?

All in all, the numbers regarding Holocaust victims are estimates, and an exact calculation is impossible. There is no way to determine precisely how many people were crammed into the cattle cars. It is only with great difficulty that one can even ascertain the number of transports traveling to the death camps from countries all across Europe.

Unloading of Jews from cars of the narrow-gauge railway in Powiercie, from whence they were transported to KL Kulmhof (Chelmno) to meet their death, 1941–42. Courtesy of the Jewish Historical Institute

To answer such a question, the usage of the word "died" must first be defined. Under Nazi occupation during World War II, Polish soldiers fighting battles, people engaged in resistance movements, victims of terror, civilians who were shelled, as well as people who were executed by the government of the Third Reich for minor crimes all "died" during the period in which the Holocaust took place. Jews made up a certain percentage of the dead in each of these categories. The term "Holocaust," however, does not refer to those losses; it refers to the systematic murder of the Jews as a nation.

In Nazi racist ideology, Jews constituted an obstacle on the path to world domination by the Aryan race and their purest core: the German

Previous page: Heap of boots belonging to victims of the Majdanek death camp; photo taken by a Soviet soldier after liberation of the camp.
Central Archives of Modern Records: the collection of the former Central Archive of the Polish United Workers' Party Central Committee

Children begging on the streets of the Warsaw Ghetto. Courtesy of the Jewish Historical Institute

nation. Jews, either as an ethnic group or as a religious group, never instigated a conflict with the Germans. They did not possess their own military power. However, these circumstances did not protect children, the elderly, or individuals baptized decades earlier from horrible persecution and bestial murder.

The Holocaust was unique among the events of World War II because of the size of the murderous campaign. The administrative government (General Government), as well as uniformed units of elite armed forces, took part in the perpetration of the Holocaust; the government and its military systematically killed Jews as part of the war. This made the Holocaust different from other aspects of World War II. That which truly distinguishes the Holocaust was the number of Jews who were murdered as well as the enormity of the campaign and the depravity of its motivations.

Among Jews, the generally accepted number of Jewish victims of the Holocaust is six million. This number is the result of calculations completed shortly after the war by Jewish sociologist and demographer Jakub Leszczynski. According to him, 5,957,000 Jews were killed in the Holocaust. Several attempts were made following this initial calculation to determine a more exact figure.

The process of calculating the exact number of Jews who were murdered in the Holocaust was generally computed as follows: The number of Jews living in a particular country prior to the beginning of the liquidation process is determined and from it is subtracted the number of Jews who survived from that country. The difference is the number of Jews murdered from each country. Statisticians, by adding up these numbers, were therefore able to calculate the number of Jews killed.

Experts disagree about the exact number of Jews because of difficulties in finding exact records. In the first edition of the *Encyclopedia of the Holocaust* (published in English, New York: Macmillan, 1990), the minimum number of Jews killed was estimated to be 5,596,000 from 22 countries; the maximum was 5,860,000. Well-known Holocaust scholar Raul Hilberg, on the other hand, calculated the number of dead as 5,100,000. His numbers—and therefore, his calculations— for the Soviet Union and Hungary were considerably understated. In the case of Poland, however, three experts—Raul Hilberg, Martin Gilbert, and Shmuel Krakowski—are in agreement that the Holocaust devoured three million of Poland's Jews.

All in all, the numbers regarding Holocaust victims are estimates, and an exact calculation is impossible. There is no way to determine precisely how many people were crammed into the cattle cars. It is only with great difficulty that one can even ascertain the number of transports traveling to the death camps from countries all across Europe.

ISRAEL GUTMAN, born in Warsaw, is a historian. He fought in the Warsaw Ghetto Uprising and was later imprisoned in Majdanek. A professor of history at the Hebrew University in Jerusalem, he is chairman of the Scientific Council of the Yad Vashem Holocaust Memorial Institute in Jerusalem. He is also the deputy chairman of the International Auschwitz Council.

ANTONY POLONSKY

▶ 5. Why did the Germans persecute the Jews?

As Jews in Germany began to ascend in economic stature, representing a large segment of the German middle class, they were resented for their new status, and anti-Semitic views developed accordingly.

Beginning in the mid-eighteenth century, a new era within Europe began to emerge. As Jews in Germany began to ascend in economic stature, representing a large segment of the German middle class, they were resented for their new status, and anti-Semitic views developed accordingly. By the end of the nineteenth century, Jewish integration came under serious attack and political anti-Semitism spread rapidly. Political anti-Semites, heavily influenced by Social Darwinian theory, rejected integration as a solution to the "Jewish Problem."

The outbreak of World War I caused hypernationalism, which in turn intensified anti-Semitic sentiment. Furthermore, with Communist revolutionaries gaining popularity throughout Europe, there was a widespread fear of a Jewish-Bolshevist conspiracy, fueled in part by the prominent role of a few Jews in the Bolshevist ranks. Lastly, following the end of violence in 1918, there was an increase in political democracy, Modernist art, literature, and music, all of which were viewed as disruptive challenges to the old conservative order, and these trends were closely linked with Jewish adherents. This compounded existing prejudices that considered Jews to be disruptive and subversive to German society. This new political anti-Semitism was ripe for exploitation by the rising Nazi Party one decade later.

The Nazi Party was able to exploit this weakness in the German democratic system to their advantage. By the end of the 1920s the Nazis drew support from the self-employed Protestant rural middle class. The National Socialists attracted many young adults who grew disillusioned with the current democratic and capitalistic institutions and who yearned for the stability and glory that had once characterized Germany. By the elections of July 1932, the Nazis had become the most popular party.

Adolf Hitler and his ilk used intimidation and political anti-Semitism to promote the party and assume power. Hitler had won the confidence of his conservative coalition allies by convincing them that he did not have a radical plan. Despite Hitler's using anti-Semitism to further his goals, the conservatives did not perceive him as radical. Rather, Hitler was viewed as a zealot for a common cause. He was able

←——————————————————————————

Previous page: German soldier cutting the *payes* (sidelocks) and beard of a young Jew cleaning the streets, probably Warsaw, 1939.
Courtesy of the Jewish Historical Institute

to prey on the rising anti-Semitism that characterized the Weimar period. Compounding anti-Semitic fears was the fact that approximately 100,000 Jews from Eastern Europe had come under German rule as a result of the war, which played into fears of growing Jewish and Russian influence. Although Hitler made no secret of his anti-Semitic views, it was not clear exactly how radical this policy was until the end of the decade.

Until 1937, his Jewish policies were kept moderate, claiming that all he was trying to achieve was to reduce the Jews' "unjustified power." To do so, the Nuremberg Laws were put in place in 1935, revoking Jewish citizenship and stripping Jews of political rights. As a result, Hitler claimed, he could fulfill the goal of enabling "the German people to arrive at a tolerable relationship toward the Jews."

Beginning with Germany's reoccupation of the Rhineland in March 1936, Hitler's policies became increasingly radicalized. The conservatives in his government were marginalized, and he made the SS dominant in security and intimidation matters. Hitler began speaking of a "fifth column" that would attack Germany from behind during the impending war. During this time Hitler pursued a barbarization of German policy, which was later reflected in his treatment of Jews

Anti-Jewish textbooks used in German schools before World War II published by Julius Streicher

German soldiers traveling to Poland in trains covered with the anti-Jewish drawings and inscriptions: "We are going to Poland to do away with the Jews." The Polish September Campaign, 1939.
Courtesy of the Jewish Historical Institute

and the Final Solution. The death penalty was introduced to apply to a wide array of offenses, and he began his euthanasia program, murdering the permanently mentally and physically handicapped, paving the way for other, broader methods of mass murder.

His Jewish policy became visibly radicalized with the invasion of Poland in 1939 and then with the invasion of the Soviet Union during Operation Barbarossa two years later. There were some instances of mass killings in Poland, although the main feature of Jewish policy at this time was the reinstitution of the walled ghetto in the East. After the failure of the Madagascar Plan (the idea of establishing French Madagascar as a penal colony for Europe's Jews) and the invasion of the Soviet Union, it became clear that Hitler was to use the cover of war to execute his policy of mass extermination. During the war, the tenet that Bolshevik equals Jew became prevalent, making it easier for soldiers and SS to consider killing Jews as part of the war effort. Once the invasion began, Hitler first promoted the use of the *Einsatzgruppen*—death squads—to accompany the front lines and murder the Jewish populations living in the newly-conquered territories. When it became apparent that this method didn't work, Hitler

German soldiers beating Jews near the synagogue.
Courtesy of the Jewish Historical Institute

promoted the introduction and use of the death camps, which, based
on the euthanasia model, resulted in the murder of most of the six
million Jews.

PROF. ANTONY POLONSKY, born in Johannesburg, is a historian who
holds the Albert Abramson Chair of Holocaust Studies, an appointment held
jointly at Brandeis University and the United States Holocaust Memorial Museum. He is author of many books and articles on Polish and Jewish history,
such as *My Brother's Keeper? Recent Polish Debates about the Holocaust* (1990).
He is also the editor of *POLIN: Studies in Polish Jewry,* of which fourteen volumes have appeared.

ISRAEL GUTMAN

▶ 6. Why did Poles collaborate with the Germans in persecuting the Jews?

One cannot claim in general terms that Poles
as a nation collaborated with the Germans
in the persecution—and therefore
in the annihilation—of Jews.
It is often thought that the vast majority
of Poles were indifferent and inactive
in the face of Jewish suffering.

One cannot claim in general terms that Poles as a nation collaborated with the Germans in the persecution—and therefore in the annihilation—of Jews. It is often thought that the vast majority of Poles were indifferent and inactive in the face of Jewish suffering. Both of these notions indifference and passivity—demand clarification and appropriate interpretation in the context of World War II and the Holocaust. One of the reasons for the lack of reaction and intervention on the part of the Polish populace was the Poles' own situation under the brutal terrors of Nazi occupation, including humiliation and enormous difficulty in fulfilling the most elementary of human needs.

One cannot, however, deny the evidence of hostility and overt expressions of joy at the suffering of the Jewish population revealed through numerous testimonies, journals, and memoirs from the period of the Holocaust. It is impossible to establish unequivocally how many people behaved in this way, but the fact remains that in the most dangerous period, those Jews who managed to force their way to the "Aryan" side but had a "bad face"—meaning a look that Poles recognized better than Germans—could not safely move through the streets of Polish cities.

Such incidents were frequent enough that one cannot explain them away as the marginal behavior of the dregs of society. Similarly, explanations claiming that a humiliated nation finds satisfaction in seeing people who are even more persecuted do not suffice to account for the phenomenon. Neither does the rising wave of anti-Semitism that occurred across Europe during this period serve as a full answer. Such repugnant behavior was far from the way in which Polish-Jewish coexistence had played itself out for centuries.

The brutal character that anti-Semitism—emerging at the beginning of the last decade of the nineteenth century—took during the Second Polish Republic, particularly during the late 1930s, played a central role. The radical right wing saw the Jews as their central enemy. The government even went so far as to seek to encourage the exodus of the majority of Jews from Poland, an action alleged as necessary for Poland's vital national interests.

Previous page: Poles (with bicycles) looking at Jews being transferred into the ghetto of Augustow. Courtesy of the Jewish Historical Institute

A letter denouncing hiding Jews. Quoted after Barbara Engelking-Boni *Szanowny panie gistapo. Donosy do władz niemieckich w Warszawie i okolicach w latach 1940–1941* (Dear Mr. Gistapo: Denunciatons to the German Authorities in Warsaw and its Vicinity in 1940-41). Institute of Philosophy and Sociology of the Polish Academy of Sciences, Warsaw, 2003

During the occupation, there were no Jewish citizens of Poland in the ranks of the government-in-exile. In the course of two years, when Jews were dying en masse from hunger and illness in the cramped confines of the ghettos, no material aid, not even a voice of solidarity, reached them from the "underground state."

The truth is that the Polish underground government sent reports to the government-in-exile in London, presenting the state of the country under occupation, including the situation of the Jews. These reports sounded an alarm that fell on deaf ears. The reports praised the Polish citizenry for their fortitude of heart and resistance to Nazi propaganda. Resistance to propaganda, however, did not include resistance to the anti-Jewish campaign. Questions must therefore be raised about the reserve and circumspection of the government in London.

Nevertheless, at the end of 1942, a group of Poles and Jews pretending to be Poles established an underground organization code-named *Zegota*. Under the leadership of members of the Provisional Committee for Aid to the Jews, democratic Catholic activists, who could not silently watch the enormity of the Nazi crimes, took part in these efforts. Such participation risked incurring the death penalty, and many Poles who helped Jews did so at the expense of their own lives.

While *szmalcowniks* (blackmailers) were the nightmare of hidden Jews, the "Righteous Among the Nations" were their angels. These were the words of Jewish historian Emanuel Ringelblum, creator of an archive of documents and diaries from the Warsaw Ghetto, who hid in a bunker on the "Aryan" side. When his secret bunker in the ghetto was discovered, Ringelblum was killed along with his whole family.

"The Righteous Among the Nations" not only saved unarmed Jews, but also the good name of their nation, along with the very notion of humanity in this bleak moment of moral collapse.

ISRAEL GUTMAN, born in Warsaw, is a historian. He fought in the Warsaw Ghetto Uprising and was later imprisoned in Majdanek. A professor of history at the Hebrew University in Jerusalem, he is chairman of the Scientific Council of the Yad Vashem Holocaust Memorial Institute in Jerusalem. He is also the deputy chairman of the International Auschwitz Council.

WLADYSLAW BARTOSZEWSKI

▶ 7. How did Poles behave during the Holocaust?

There can be no discussion of a uniform
or identical pattern of behavior by Polish people
under the changing conditions of the occupation,
during different phases of World War II,
and in the different residential situations.
The vast majority of the population
was immobilized by fear of survival
and the battle for everyday existence
under conditions of intense Nazi terror.

Wladyslaw Bartoszewski
Courtesy of the Jewish Historical
Institute

Jan Karski, courier of the Polish
government-in-exile, declared an honorary citizen of Israel and a Righteous
Among the Nations by Yad Vashem.
Courtesy of the Jewish Historical Institute

Out of approximately 22 million Poles (the Polish national population—including children—within the borders of the Polish state as
configured at the moment of Hitler's attack on Poland on September
1, 1939), more than a million found themselves in German captivity
and at least half were deported, at Stalin's orders, from Poland's eastern territories (eight provinces) into the heart of the Soviet Union, at
the moment when visible acts of extermination of the Jewish population began in the spring of 1942. Approximately one third of Poles lived
on terrain that by October 1939 had already been forcibly annexed to
the German Third Reich, in violation of international law. These people
were deprived of all civil rights, subject to very severe orders, hard labor,
and continual repression on any pretext. They were, in sum, practically
prisoners.

Two thirds of Poles—those in the five administrative areas (Cracow,
Warsaw, Radom, Lublin, and Lvov) in the central and southern Polish
territories (in total, around 14 million men, women, and children)—
lived under the so-called General Government, led by Hans Frank, who
was executed in 1946 by the Americans at Nuremberg for committing
mass crimes against Jews and Poles between autumn 1939 and Janu-

Previous page: Crowd looking on as a woman is punished by the Germans for
trading with Jews, Grybow, 1941. Courtesy of the Jewish Historical Institute

Polish woman who sold food to Jews. The punishment for trade with Jews was death penalty. Courtesy of the Jewish Historical Institute

Jan Kostanski (left), a Polish Christian teenager who, during the German occupation, on a daily basis assisted Jews in the ghetto and hid, with his mother, a Jewish family. He sits on a bench in Saski Park with his Jewish friend Wladek Cykiert, Warsaw, 1940.
Courtesy of USHMM

ary 1945. In 1942 Hans Frank and his subordinate district governors announced a "decree" that threatened with death all those who dared offer help in any form to Jews, who were by then mostly isolated in or escaping from ghettos. This decree was, in fact, carried out, and its victims included at least a few thousand people, often entire families, who had offered shelter to Jews.

There can be no discussion of a uniform or identical pattern of behavior by Polish people under the changing conditions of the occupation, during different phases of World War II, and in the different residential situations in regions incorporated into the General Government (i.e., big cities, small cities, towns, and the countryside). The vast majority of the population was immobilized by fear of survival and the battle for everyday existence under conditions of intense Nazi terror. These issues forced all other matters to become lesser priorities. Poles wished the worst upon the German occupiers, and each of their misfortunes was celebrated. For example, the armed Jewish youth resistance in the Warsaw Ghetto in April and May of 1943 was generally viewed by Poles with approval and respect; there is documentation of active aid given by Poles to the fugitives.

Poland was the only nation in German-occupied Europe to have had, from the very first weeks of the war, its own fully official president in Western Europe, initially in France, and from June 1940 in

War portrait of Irena Sendler, nominated for the Nobel Peace Prize for her rescue of Jews from the Warsaw Ghetto. In December 1942 she was appointed by the Council to Aid the Jews to head its children's department. As an employee of the Social Welfare Department, she had a permit to enter the Warsaw Ghetto and cooperated with the Polish Relief Organization. She organized the smuggling of Jewish children from the ghetto and saved approximately 2,500 lives. Arrested in 1943 by the Gestapo, she was tortured and sentenced to death, but rescued by *Zegota*, she continued her work in hiding. She was recognized as a Righteous Among the Nations by Yad Vashem. Courtesy of the Jewish Historical Institute

Great Britain. The Polish government in London and the commanders of the Polish armed forces—subordinate to the Allies—residing there presented an unequivocal position regarding the behavior of Polish citizens vis-à-vis their occupiers. The guidelines of the Polish government, endowed with significant authority in the occupied country, were disseminated throughout the population by a secret civil and military center (the Government Delegate's Office at Home) from February 1942, the commander of the Home Army (formerly the Association of Armed Struggle), and were mediated by the underground press. Through their proclamations and announcements, the government advocated giving active aid to persecuted Jews and, at the same time, systematically informed the governments of Great Britain, the United States, and other countries of the Free World about the increasing threat to the continued existence of Jews on occupied terrain, and later of their successive extermination.

Secret emissaries and couriers escaped, with great difficulty, from occupied Poland to England with alarming information and documents on this topic. The best known of these couriers was Jan Karski (then an officer in the Home Army and after the war a professor at Georgetown University in Washington for many years), who left occupied Warsaw in October of 1942 and reached London at the beginning of November of the same year. A document of key significance was a note dated December 10, 1942, from the Polish government in London to the governments of the nations waging war against Germany, entitled "The Mass Extermination of Jews in German Occupied Poland." It resulted in the historic declaration by twelve Allied nations on December 17, 1942, "Concerning Responsibility for the Extermination of the Jews."

From the fall of 1942 the Council for Jewish Aid was active in occupied Poland—at first only in Warsaw, but later in Cracow and Lvov—through the Government Delegate's Office. The council was an interparty organization, coordinating various preexisting initiatives and activities, for example, the long-standing effort to rescue children organized by a group of lawyers of the Municipal Administration in Warsaw, led by Irena Sendler. Paralleling the already challenging attempts to save people was a dangerous phenomenon of blackmail and denunciation of hidden Jews. The independent Polish underground government emphatically denounced this practice; a series of death sentences were pronounced, especially in Warsaw and Cracow, regarding this type of criminal behavior, but the phenomenon of blackmail undoubtedly impeded efforts at help because it increased intimidation: Along with Jews, Poles who found the courage to help them also fell victim to denunciation.

Sixty years after the war, at the end of 2004, the Yad Vashem Institute in Jerusalem (the Holocaust Martyrs and Heroes Remembrance Authority of the State of Israel) has recognized almost 6,000 Poles, individuals or entire families, as "Righteous Among the Nations," those who saved Jews at the risk of their own lives. There is not, however, any credible and accurate documentation of the activities of criminals. In any case, all the political and social powers in occupied Poland similarly assessed the German crimes against the Jews to be a willful and planned genocide.

PROF. WLADYSLAW BARTOSZEWSKI is a historian, former Polish minister of foreign affairs, co-founder of the Polish *Zegota* Council for Aid to Jews, holder of the Righteous Among the Nations distinction, participant in the Warsaw Uprising of 1944, and former prisoner of KL Auschwitz. He is also the director of the International Auschwitz Council for the Polish Government, and an honorary citizen of the State of Israel.

WLADYSLAW BARTOSZEWSKI

▸ 8. How could it be that Poles let the Germans build ghettos and concentration camps in their neighborhoods?

The Polish population had not the slightest influence on the selection of sites of terror against Polish Christians, nor on the places of deportation and extermination of Jews, and found out the basic facts about them only after significant delay.

First of all, under occupation, Poles had nothing to say about the intentions and activities of their occupiers, and in contrast to occupied countries in Western Europe, they did not have even a makeshift government or authorized institution on their home territory representing the population. Secondly, the tactics of Nazi terror in occupied Poland anticipated the full isolation of Jews from non-Jews (according to the Nuremberg racial criteria) during the first two years of occupation, through the creation of a separate, closed living area for Jews. The Nazis destroyed any will to resist on the part of Poles through the extermination of their elites—through secret mass executions of teachers, priests, lawyers, political and community activists, and officers, or their exile to concentration camps.

The Germans opened Auschwitz I—the first large concentration camp on the territory of the prewar Polish state—in the spring of 1940, and from mid-June of that year until the end of the occupation, they placed Polish political prisoners there; in total, almost 100,000 Polish Christians died there. After the decision for the "Final Solution of the Jewish Question" in January 1942, the Central Office for Reich Security ("Reichsicherheitshauptamt"/RSHA) began directing transports of Jews to the newly-constructed affiliate, Auschwitz II-Birkenau, first from the nearby territories of Slovakia, and then from France, Germany, and other countries. Polish prisoners in Auschwitz could not have had (and did not have) any influence whatsoever on these developments, and the Polish population from the area adjacent to the camp was either forciby deported to the Reich or resettled to the east.

A similar situation occurred with the creation of the Majdanek concentration camp. In the fall of 1941, the Germans established a camp for prisoners of war on the outskirts of the provincial city of Lublin, designated, after the outbreak of the German-Soviet War, for captured soldiers. During 1942-43 Jews and Polish political prisoners were taken to the camp. On-site mass executions, especially of Jewish prisoners, were carried out in November 1942. But numerous Polish Christians, including Catholic priests, were also killed at Majdanek.

Previous page: Polish and Jewish workers building a wall to separate the Warsaw Ghetto from the "Aryan" part of the city (November 1940–June 1941). Courtesy of USHMM

Life on both sides of the wall of the Warsaw Ghetto along Grzybowska Street,
June 1942.
Courtesy of the Jewish Historical Institute

Tram marked with a Star of David approaching the gate of the Warsaw Ghetto
on Grzybowska Street, Warsaw, 1941.
Courtesy of the Jewish Historical Institute

Other sites of the Jewish Holocaust well-known today, in which more than one and a half million people were murdered, are Treblinka, Sobibor, and Belzec. In each case the extermination centers (not concentration camps) were situated in the forest, far away from larger cities and centers of civilization, on military terrain generally inaccessible to the Polish population. This deliberate attempt by the Germans to hide the sites of mass crimes certainly impeded obtaining information about them.

Nevertheless, after some time—although belatedly—news of the extermination reached both the Polish resistance movement and activists from the Jewish underground organizations in the Warsaw Ghetto. Isolated individuals also managed to escape during transports to the extermination centers, and even from the extermination center of Treblinka itself, where the Germans murdered the majority of the Jewish population of Warsaw.

The Polish population had not the slightest influence on the selection of sites of terror against Polish Christians, nor on the places of deportation and extermination of Jews, and found out the basic facts about them only after significant delay, through periodicals of the Polish underground press published by the resistance movement authorized in London.

PROF. WLADYSLAW BARTOSZEWSKI is a historian, former Polish minister of foreign affairs, co-founder of the Polish *Zegota* Council for Aid to Jews, holder of the Righteous Among the Nations distinction, participant in the Warsaw Uprising of 1944, and former prisoner of KL Auschwitz. He is also the director of the International Auschwitz Council for the Polish Government, and an honorary citizen of the State of Israel.

TOMASZ SZAROTA

▸ 9. Did Poles organize anti-Jewish pogroms during World War II?

Everywhere anti-Jewish activities were undertaken—with the support of the German occupiers—by prewar groups of the political radical right. The Germans rewarded the participants with vodka and money. The violence was filmed for use in German propaganda, to demonstrate the anti-Semitism of the Poles and to make the Germans appear as defenders of the Jews against the savage crowds.

Were the question posed as, "During World War II, were there cases where Poles were active participants in the German extermination of Jews, and even themselves killed Jews?" then, unfortunately, the answer would be in the affirmative. But if the question concerns organized pogroms, meaning preplanned undertakings that only gave an outward impression of being spontaneous, the answer would be significantly more complicated and limited. I base this on my own analysis of comparable events that took place on the streets of Warsaw, Paris, Amsterdam, The Hague, Antwerp, and Kovno in the years 1940-41, as described in the book *On the Threshold of the Holocaust: Anti-Jewish Riots and Pogroms in Occupied Europe.* Where the Germans were not the organizers of the pogroms, they were certainly often their inspiration, although in one case—Kovno— it is fully documented.

Everywhere rioters included local people. And everywhere anti-Jewish activities were undertaken—with the support of the German occupiers—by prewar groups of the political radical right. The Warsaw pogrom took place not only under German control and with the support of the occupying government (the Germans rewarded the participants with vodka and money), but the violence was filmed for use in German propaganda, to demonstrate the anti-Semitism of the Poles and to make the Germans appear as defenders of the Jews against the savage crowds. The Polish underground press condemned the pogrom—in which, it should be stressed, no victims were mortally wounded—and published the names of Poles known to have been the co-organizers, branding them as traitors in service to the occupiers, and treating the pogrom itself as a German provocation.

The events in Radzilow and Jedwabne, as well as in other towns in Polish regions which were under the Soviet occupation during 1939-1941 and then went over to the rule of a new, this time German, occupation should be seen, in my opinion, as the realization of the objectives imposed by the Operational Group of the Security Police and the Security Services under the control of the government of the Nazi Third Reich. After June 22, 1941, in the occupied areas, one of the most significant goals of the *Einsatzgruppen* was the institution of the so-called "self-cleansing actions" (*Selbstreinigungsaktionen*)—that is, the Nazis organized anti-Jewish pogroms which were planned to give the impression of being spontaneous outbreaks of "popular wrath" or "settling of old scores" by the local population with their "Jewish oppressors." In his report of October 15, 1941, SS Brigadeführer Walter Stahlecker wrote cynically: "It was no less

← **Previous page:** Twins Mordechaj Menachem and Jaakow Cwi Zylbersztejn, in the 1930s, killed in the Radzilow pogrom on July 7,1941. All photos in this chapter are from Jose Gutstein collection / www.radzilow.com

59

Sara Zimnowicz née Gutstein and her husband, Jakob Zimnowicz, killed with their eight-year-old daughter Szulamit in Radzilow on July 7, 1941.

The Zylbersztajn and Jonkac siblings. All were killed on July 7, 1941.

Rywka Gelgor née Grajewska, killed on July 7, 1941.

Pesza Gutsztejn née Zimnowicz, killed on July 7, 1941.

Rabbi Jehoszua Zelig Gelgor, killed in Radzilow on July 7, 1941.

Mordechaj Grubawicz, the 1930s, killed on July 7, 1941.

important to create facts that were both clear and that would be provable at a future date, testifying that the local population, when unleashed, themselves came up with the harshest measures against the Bolsheviks and Jewish enemies of their own accord, in contrast to which recommendations given by the German side would be barely identifiable."

Jan Tomasz Gross in his book *Neighbors* made a false assumption that on 10 July, 1941, in the Lomza region, where Jedwabne is situated, there were no longer any formations of the Operational Group. The detailed research carried out by the Institute of National Memory after the publication of Gross's book and published in a two-volume work entitled *Wokół Jedwabnego* (Around Jedwabne) containing over a thousand pages allows us to state that the murders committed on Jews in Radzilow and Jedwabne—and, as it turned out, also in other towns of this region in summer 1941—were inspired by the Germans, but perpetrated by the Poles.

It must be remembered that the authorities of the Polish government-in-exile presiding in London anticipated that the Germans would attempt to instigate Poles to engage in anti-Jewish excesses. In instructions on June 23, 1941, directed to the country just before the outbreak of the German-Soviet war, the premier of this government, General Wladyslaw Sikorski, wrote, "The government places great emphasis on the necessity of warning society not to succumb to the German instigators of excesses against Jews in the areas liberated from Soviet occupation." By July 1941, however, it was no longer possible to transmit these instructions to the Lomza region, because the local structure of the Polish underground had already been crushed by the NKVD (Soviet Secret Police).

A few months later, when news reached Warsaw that it had not been possible to prevent Polish participation in the murder of Jews, in *Prawda*, a paper published by an underground Catholic organization, an editorial appeared: "We must work to prevent similar disgraces with all available means. We must inform the people that they are becoming Herod's assasins, condemn the murderers in the underground press, call to boycott and threaten them, and warn of the severe judgment by the free Republic. In no way can we accept the contagion of bestiality and sadism that would infect us."

TOMASZ SZAROTA is a historian, professor of the Historical Institute at the Polish Academy of Sciences, and expert on the history of World War II and the Nazi occupation, as well as on national stereotypes. He is the author of a number of books including *Okupowanej Warszawy dzień powszedni* (Everyday Life in Occupied Warsaw), 1978, *Niemiecki Michel* (German Michel), 1990, and *U progu Zagłady. Zajścia antyżydowskie i pogromy w okupowanej Europie* (Portents of Annihilation: Anti-Jewish Riots and Pogroms in Occupied Europe), 2000.

LEON KIERES

▶ 10. What really happened at Jedwabne?

A complete answer to the question of the events that took place in the town of Jedwabne on July 10, 1941, will probably never be possible. The poor state of archival documentation, as well as the fact that the majority of the witnesses are no longer living, does not allow us to fully clarify the circumstances of the crime. We know, however, that on July 10, 1941, with encouragement from the German government, a part of the Jewish population numbering at least 340 people were killed by the local population.

A complete answer to the question of the events that took place in the town of Jedwabne on July 10, 1941, will probably never be possible. The poor state of archival documentation, as well as the fact that the majority of the witnesses are no longer living, does not allow us to fully clarify the circumstances of the crime. The fourth consecutive investigation of the incident (under the Communist government three investigations were carried out, of which two ended in guilty verdicts), undertaken by the Institute of National Memory from September 2000 to June 2003, helped to establish many new facts, as well as correcting some mistaken conclusions. However, to a significant extent the events of Jedwabne some sixty-three years ago remain more in the realm of hypothesis than prosecutorial knowledge.

Nonetheless, from the proceedings of the investigation led by Radoslaw Ignatiew, procurator of the Institute of National Memory, we know that on July 10, 1941, with encouragement from the German government, a part of the Jewish population numbering at least 340 people were killed by the local population. The crime was committed in two stages. First, a group of 40-50 men were murdered and their bodies buried inside a barn belonging to Bronislaw Sleszynski. Next, approximately 300 men and women of different ages, including children and infants, were burned alive in that same barn. The number of approximately 340 people is not precise, because, first, the number is based on estimates made by the archeological-anthropological team that did the exhumation work, and secondly, we know that individual murders took place in other settings. Thus, the actual number of victims is certainly larger. Strictly speaking, the direct murderers were ethnic Polish men, numbering at least forty, coming both from Jedwabne itself and nearby villages. The massacre was undoubtedly arranged in advance, because already on the day before the events local peasants came to the town with plans to steal Jewish property; there were also instances of warnings given to Jews by their Polish neighbors about an anticipated pogrom. The next day, after the Jewish inhabitants were burned in the barn, general looting of Jewish property took place. Every Jew whom the mob could lay their hands upon perished.

It must be emphasized that to broaden our knowledge about what happened at Jedwabne, the events discussed must be placed in the context of the military, political, and demographic situation of the entire

---

Previous page: Road sign in Jedwabne. Photo by B. Osser

Aleksander Kwasniewski, the president of Poland, and Shevach Weiss, Israeli ambassador to Poland, during the commemoration of the sixtieth anniversary of the mass murder in Jedwabne, on July 10, 2001. Photo by C. Fissel

region of Jedwabne at the time. The outbreak of the German-Soviet war and the invasion of this region by Hitler's army created chaos and intensified criminality, as is typical during a state of war; it empowered the Polish anti-Communist underground, which was decimated by the Soviet security forces. For many members of the underground, the German invasion meant freedom from Soviet bondage, as well as the opportunity to get even with actual or imagined Soviet collaborators and to avenge personal injustices, above all the deportations of their peers into the depths of the Soviet Union. The Jewish population was accused of collaborating with the Soviet regime, and thus of disloyalty to the Polish state. These accusations were in part true, although in part without foundation; they were based on the Jewish population's observed preference at finding themselves under the Soviet regime (which, in comparison with the Nazi invasion, which came accompanied by the broadcasting of radically anti-Semitic slogans, was less of a threat to their self-preservation) rather than any factual evidence of Jewish collaboration with the Soviets. Nevertheless, in the local consciousness, Jews, as the only significant ethnic minority in the region besides Poles, were identified as supporters of Communism, and the hatred of Soviet collaborators easily was vented on the local Jewish population.

In this situation, the German security forces found, among the Polish population demoralized by the war, people eager to collaborate on an anti-Jewish pretext. In Jedwabne a key role was played by people who were known (or thought) to be *volksdeutsch* (ethnic Germans), such as Karol Bardon or Marian Karolak—the latter was the leader of the group of murderers. Few traces of archival documentation remained regarding the measures taken by the German security police, because its functionaries were instructed to act in a way that gave the impression that the local population took revenge on the Jews on its own initiative and under its own power.

German engagement in the crime, at least at the level of inspiration and consent, is indisputable. One of the commanding officers of the German police operating during those days in the Jedwabne region, Hermann Schaper, was recognized in a photograph by surviving Jews. Likewise, the very sequence of the murders in Jedwabne suggests German inspiration. The gathering of people in the main square, the order to clean the square, the abuse of victims accompanied by ceremonial smashing of Soviet monuments, forced singing, and parades with the Soviet flag during which Jews "confessed" to being guilty of starting the war were all well-known German scenarios preceding the murder of Jews across East-Central Europe. Similarly, the burning of the victims in the barn was a common element of the Germans' scenario—not, it should be noted, in relation only to the Jewish population.

The Institute of National Memory has been charged with addressing, by legal means, crimes committed against citizens of the Polish state, regardless of their ethnicity. In this case crimes were committed against our Jewish compatriots. Therefore, we insist upon the same measures being taken regarding their memory, pursuing, if possible, the perpetrators in the name of the Polish state, which—had it existed at that time—certainly would have not left the crimes unpunished.

LEON KIERES is a law professor at Wroclaw University and a former senator in the Polish Parliament (1997-2000). Since 1990 a member of the local government in Wroclaw, he represented Poland in the Local and Regional Authorities Congress of the European Council (1992-2004). He was a European Council observer at the local elections in Croatia (1997) and municipal elections in Bosnia and Herzegovina (1998) and is former president of the Institute of National Memory (2000-05).

Maciej Kozlowski

▸ 11. Did Poles save Jews during the Holocaust?

Yad Vashem, Israel's Holocaust Memorial and educational center, estimates that between 20,000 and 40,000 people were saved in this manner. Other sources give higher numbers, typically between 50,000 and 100,000. Given the postwar survival statistics, I think the figure of 50,000 to 60,000 saved on the Aryan side is closest to the truth.

Yes. It is an indisputable fact that many Poles, at the risk of not only their own lives, but the lives of their family and friends, helped to hide Jews during the war, thus saving them from death. The debate revolves rather around the extent of this help and also—creating the most controversy—whether the help given was effective, and whether, under the conditions of the occupation, it might have been possible to do more.

First, the numbers: Before the war, inside the Polish Republic lived approximately 3,500,000 Jews of Polish citizenship. Among them about 350,000-400,000 survived. Around three-fourths of this group at most were saved inside the Soviet Union; surely a small number managed to escape to the West during the first months of the war, and certainly another small portion survived the death camps. The rest survived in hiding, thanks to the help of their Polish fellow citizens. Of course, during the war, no one kept statistics on how many people were being saved. The data presented in historical research projects vary greatly. Yad Vashem, Israel's Holocaust Memorial and educational center, estimates that between 20,000 and 40,000 people were saved in this manner. Other sources give higher numbers, typically between 50,000 and 100,000. Given the postwar survival statistics, I think the figure of 50,000 to 60,000 saved on the Aryan side is closest to the truth.

Under the conditions of the occupation, to offer help and shelter to a single person in hiding required the participation—and putting at risk—of at least ten or more people. Such actions endangered the lives not only of those who themselves took people into hiding, but also the lives of all those who knew about the hidden Jews. In Poland, under the orders imposed by the occupying administration, not only providing any help to Jews was punishable by death, but merely not informing the authorities about hidden Jews was punishable by deportation to a concentration camp—typically, meaning death. It was very rarely possible to keep a person in hiding in a single apartment; generally, it was necessary to change locations periodically. In the case of someone hiding "on Aryan papers," the papers had to be falsified and any trace that could lead to discovery of the truth also had to be eradicated. There were cases, of course, when the same people helped many Jews. On the

---

←

Previous page: Sister Jadwiga with a group under her care in the cloister in Lomna, where Jewish children were hidden, Lomna, 1942.
Courtesy of USHMM

Abraham Grinbaum with Helena Grabarek, a Polish woman who hid him for three years, in a village near Gabin, during World War II.
Courtesy of the Jewish Historical Institute

Henryk Slawik, Polish journalist and activist in the Polish Socialistic Party. As a representative of the Ministry of Labor of the Polish government-in-exile, he organized help for refugees and facilitated escape to the West. In cooperation with the representative of the Hungarian government, Jozsef Antall, Sr., he issued documents to the refugees. Thanks to Slawik and his associates, documents saving the lives of a few thousand Jews were issued. Arrested in 1944 after the Germans overran Hungary, he took all guilt on himself and was murdered in the Nazi death camp in Mauthausen.

Rytm: *Polski Wallenberg. Rzecz o Henryku Sławiku* (Polish Wallenberg. About Henryk Slawik)

other hand, it is unknown how many Polish non-Jews never admitted they helped Jews because those whom they tried to help perished. Also unknown is the number of those who were killed for sheltering Jews. Providing numbers is therefore risky. But with all these reservations, let us make such an attempt.

Thus, if we accept the lower number of ten people helping each hidden Jew, and the midrange number of fifty thousand people saved, we arrive at the number of half a million Poles actively engaged in helping their fellow citizens who were condemned to death. Maybe there were not as many as that. Nevertheless, we are talking about tens or hundreds of thousands of people, not mere thousands. Considering that the size of the population under the control of the General Government—where, in practice, the largest number of Jews were hidden—was twelve and a half million people, that means almost five percent of Polish society participated in rescuing.

The delicate issue remains: What were the motives of those who helped? The Yad Vashem Institute regards as Righteous Among the Nations only those who helped without taking any financial reward. It is known that many helped freely, without return. But there were cases where help was offered for money. Even so, under the reality of the

The Ulma family from Markowa: The parents and six children were shot, together with the Szall and Goldman families whom they were hiding (eight people). The Catholic Church recommended their beatification.
M. Szpytma collection

Dr. Jan Zabinski, director of the Warsaw Zoo. During the occupation he was appointed superintendent of the city's public parks, a position he used to avail himself of the opportunity to visit the Warsaw Ghetto. He got in touch with his prewar Jewish friends and helped them escape and find shelter on the "Aryan" side of the city. After the September Campaign, many cages in the zoo were emptied of animals and Zabinski utilized them as hiding places for fleeing Jews. An active member of the Home Army (Armia Krajowa), Zabinski participated in the Warsaw Uprising of 1944. He was taken prisoner and sent to Germany. His wife, Antonina, and his son, Ryszard, continued his work of rescuing Jews. In 1968 he was recognized as one of the Righteous Among the Nations by Yad Vashem. Courtesy of USHMM

occupation, strict distinction between these cases was difficult. Now, decades later, it seems impossible. When can taking rent for an apartment where Jews were hidden be called a motive of greed and when must it be seen as providing for a bare necessity? The impoverished Polish population under occupation also fought for survival.

Nevertheless, Poland, among the countries where the Nazis carried out their plan of extermination, differed not only in the scale of help offered to Jews and in the draconian punishments applied by the Germans, but also in the institutionalization of aid on the governmental level. On September 27, 1942, at the initiative of underground Catholic and federal organizations, the Konrad Zegota Provisional Committee to Aid Jews was established. On December 4 of that year, the Council for Aid to Jews was formed and run by the Polish government-in-exile. The council took the cryptonym Zegota. Zegota had branches in Cracow and Lvov and within the local department in charge of the remaining areas of Poland. A significant part of the budget of the underground state went to help in hiding Jews. In 1943 this was almost five million zlotys, and in 1944 some tens of millions. Zegota had a variety of departments, of which the most important were: the department of housing, charged with finding shelter for those in hiding; the children's department, directed by Irena Sendler; and the legal, medical, and propaganda

OGŁOSZENIE

Dotyczy:

przetrzymywania ukrywających się żydów.

Zachodzi potrzeba przypomnienia, że stosownie do § 3 Rozporządzenia o ograniczeniach pobytu w Gen. Gub. z dnia 15. X. 1941 roku (Dz. Rozp. dla GG. str. 595) żydzi, opuszczający dzielnicę żydowską bez zezwolenia, podlegają karze śmierci.

Według tego rozporządzenia, osobom, które takim żydom świadomie udzielają przytułku, dostarczają im jedzenia lub sprzedają artykuły żywnościowe, grozi również kara śmierci.

Niniejszym ostrzega się stanowczo ludność nieżydowską przed:

1.) udzielaniem żydom przytułku,

2.) dostarczaniem im jedzenia,

3.) sprzedawaniem im artykułów żywnościowych.

Częstochowa, dnia 24. 9. 42.

Proclamation warning Poles of the death penalty to be meted out to those supporting Jews in any way in the territory of the General Government, September 1942. Courtesy of the Jewish Historical Institute

departments. The council also took action against blackmailers. In total, during two-and-a-half years of activity, the council provided help for a few thousand Jews, who, without this help, would not have been able to survive.

An important aspect of assistance offered by the state government during the entire period of the occupation was informing the Allies of the fate of the Jewish people and making repeated appeals for help. The most publicized of these efforts was the mission of Polish courier Jan Karski, who in the fall of 1942 reached London carrying a detailed report on the extent of the extermination taking place on Polish soil. Karski, wanting to be specifically and personally acquainted with the circumstances of the ongoing extermination of the Jewish people, went twice in disguise into the ghetto and also sneaked into the extermination camp at Belzec in the uniform of an Estonian guard. He presented his dramatic personal testimony to the British and American governments, and to Franklin D. Roosevelt himself. His written account, *The Story of a Secret State*, which appeared in print in 1944, was intended to shock the conscience of the world and lead to a change in Allied policy—although we know this did not come to pass. To protest against the indifference of the world, Szmul Zygielbojm, one of Karski's interlocutors and the Bund's representative to the National Council (a makeshift Polish parliament in London), committed suicide.

A separate chapter in the history of Polish aid to Jews was the help given to the fighters of the Warsaw Ghetto. The Polish underground delivered some arms to the organized Jewish resistance movement. The Jewish Fighting Organization received 70 pistols with ammunition, one submachine gun, one squad machine gun, and a significant number of grenades and explosive materials. On a larger scale, a segment of the Home Army Security Corps is believed to have armed the Jewish Military Union, although this has not been documented. During the fighting in the ghetto, some diversionary actions took place at the walls. These actions, whose goal was to create a breach in the wall to enable the civilian population of the ghetto to escape, were unsuccessful. In the course of this operation, a few soldiers of the Polish underground were killed.

The last significant act of help to the Jews took place during the Warsaw Uprising. One of the troops of the Zoska battalion, after a daring action, freed over three hundred Jewish prisoners in the Gesiowka camp, which remained on the ruins of the former ghetto.

In recognition for their help given to Jews, almost 6,000 Poles were decorated by the State of Israel with medals designating them "Righteous Among the Nations." Poles are nearly one third of all those so honored.

There remains, of course, the eternal question: Could more have been done? To such a question, Wladyslaw Bartoszewski once answered that all aid is always insufficient, especially in a situation of a powerful catastrophe like the Holocaust. The only people who did as much as they possibly could were those who gave their lives trying to help. And there were hundreds of such Poles—maybe even thousands.

The terrible tragedy remains, of course, that alongside the heroes who endangered their own lives every day to help those most threatened were many others who profited from their fellow citizens' misfortune, blackmailing hidden Jews. Despite the appeals of the Polish underground and the death sentences brought down on such *szmalcowniks* (as the blackmailers were called), this plague was pervasive, and without question, significantly more could have been done, as it was not condemned as strongly as other forms of collaboration.

Approximately 25 percent of the Polish population took part in one or another form of underground activity. That help for Jews was not as common as other forms of resistance was influenced not only by the draconian punishments ruthlessly applied by the Germans, but undoubtedly also by the anti-Semitic atmosphere, widespread in Polish society as well as in the resistance movement. Therefore many Poles who helped Jews during the occupation were afraid to admit it even after the war. The general brutalization of life was also a significant factor. It should be recognized that the extreme poverty and starvation experienced by the entire population made giving any form of help to another person much more difficult.

And a final point: The massive Jewish population in Poland was largely isolated from Polish society, differing in language, culture, and custom. For the vast majority of Polish Jews who died during the Holocaust, any form of local aid was completely impossible. On the other hand, on a larger scale, a change in Allied policy would have been possible. Despite dramatic appeals by the Polish underground and the Polish government, that policy was never changed. For the Allies, rescuing the Jews dying in the Holocaust never became a military priority.

DR. MACIEJ KOZLOWSKI is a historian, diplomat, former ambassador of the Republic of Poland to Israel, and former Polish deputy minister of foreign affairs.

FELIKS TYCH

▸ 12. Why didn't Jews fight back against the Germans during World War II?

This question is based upon incorrect information and reflects myth rather than actual history.

In every persecuted society in occupied Europe, there were people who fought and others—constituting the majority—who were passive. This was true among the Jews as well. They should be judged no differently—and furthermore one should bear in mind that Jews lived under conditions of persecution and displacement that made active resistance significantly more difficult during the war.

Marek Edelman – the last surviving leader of the Warsaw Ghetto Uprising. Photo by A. Rozanski

This question is based upon incorrect information and reflects myth rather than actual history. In every persecuted society in occupied Europe, there were people who fought and others—constituting the majority—who were passive. This was true among the Jews as well. They should be judged no differently—and furthermore one should bear in mind that Jews lived under conditions of persecution and displacement that made active resistance significantly more difficult during the war.

Polish Jews fought back against the Germans. In the campaign of September 1939, the number of fallen Jewish soldiers was proportional to the number of Jews in the country's general population. The Warsaw Ghetto Uprising from April 19 to May 17, 1943, was the first revolt against the occupiers on Polish territory; armed incidents also took place in the ghettos in Bialystok (in February and August 1943), Czestochowa, Bedzin, and other places. Jews even fought in the labor, concentration, and extermination camps, with uprisings in Treblinka on August 2, 1943; in Sobibor on October 14, 1943; and in Auschwitz on October 7, 1944.

Previous page: Group of Jewish partisans under the command of Abba Kovner, near Vilna, World War II. Courtesy of the Jewish Historical Institute

Janina Krzeminska (left) and Bluma Zylbcrgcr, nuises of the Polish "Anders Army," in a hospital in Tehran. The Anders Army was composed in 1942 of Poles released from Soviet prisons and labor camps. General Wladyslaw Anders evacuated 160,000 Poles from Russia through Persia, Palestine, and Egypt. In January 1944 they landed in Italy as part of the British 8th Army and continued the fight on the continent.
Courtesy of Shalom Golda Tencer-Szurmiej Foundation

They fought as well in partisan divisions, both self-formed groups (especially in the eastern regions and in the General Government), and with armed organizations like the AK ("Home Army"), AL ("People's Army"), and the PAL ("Polish People's Army"). They also fought in Soviet partisan units. They took part in the Warsaw Uprising of 1944 among the ranks of the AK and AL, sustaining great losses. They fought in all of the anti-Nazi coalition armies. Proportional to their numbers, Jewish participation in the fight against the Germans on the African and European fronts during World War II was no less than any other ethnic group, and often it was larger. An additional form of resistance against the criminal plans of the Nazi occupiers was the phenomenon of Jews hiding on the "Aryan" side, in defiance of German orders.

Myths of Jewish passivity already began emerging during the years of the occupation, based on the fact that Jews generally went to the death transports without displays of armed resistance. But many factors accounted for this phenomenon. The Jews were practically unarmed. Only with immense difficulty did they acquire individual pieces of weaponry from the Polish underground, and generally Jews were not accepted into most Polish partisan formations. The negligible resistance exhibited by the majority of Jews against deportation resulted from the way the Nazis masked their plans to murder the Jews

Warszawa, ghetto 23 kwietnia 1943 r. *1*

Polacy, Obywatele, Żołnierze Wolności!

Wśród huku armat, z których armia niemiecka wali do naszych domów, do mieszkań naszych matek, dzieci i żon;
Wśród terkotu karabinów maszynowych, które zdobywamy w walce na tchórzliwych żandarmach i S.S.-owcach
Wśród pożarów i kurzu krwi mordowanego ghetta Warszawy - my - więźniowie ghetta - ślemy Wam bratnie, serdeczne pozdrowienia.
Wiemy, że w serdecznym bólu i łzach współczucia, że z podziwem i trwogą o wynik tej walki przyglądacie się wojnie, jaką od wielu dni toczymy z okrutnym okupantem.
Lecz wiedzcie także, że każdy próg ghetta jak dotychczas, tak i nadal będzie twierdzą; że może wszyscy zginiemy w walce, lecz nie poddamy się; że dyszymy, jak i Wy, żądzą odwetu i kary za wszystkie zbrodnie wspólnego wroga!
Toczy się walka o Waszą i naszą Wolność!
O Wasz i nasz - ludzki, społeczny, narodowy - honor i godność!
Pomścimy zbrodnie Oświęcimia, Treblinki, Bełżca, Majdanka!
Niech żyje braterstwo broni i krwi Walczącej Polski!
Niech żyje Wolność!
Śmierć katom i oprawcom!
Niech żyje walka na śmierć i życie z okupantem!

ŻYDOWSKA ORGANIZACJA BOJOWA.

Appeal of the Jewish Fighting Organization to the Warsaw community, on April 23, 1943, made during the battle in the Warsaw Ghetto.
Courtesy of the Jewish Historical Institute

by carefully disguising the destinations of deportation transports as "work centers in the East." The monstrosity of the German crimes was so inconceivable and illogical—disposing of a badly needed, "free" slave labor force—that it was conducive to fostering the illusion among Jews, right up to the end, that the majority would survive if they contributed through "work." Even the Allies, when they received information about the industrial killing of Jews, listened with disbelief and undertook no military efforts to halt the murder.

The situation of Jews during World War II was determined by three objective elements:

1) **Power relations:** Almost entirely deprived of weapons, the Jewish population had no chance of effectively confronting the German military machine. By analogy, the Germans resettled approximately 1.5 million Poles from Polish territory incorporated into the Reich onto the terrain of the General Government. This deportation was not accompanied by any cases of collective resistance,

Tomasz Toivi Blatt, one of the participants in the Jewish prisoner revolt in the Sobibor concentration camp in 1943. Photo by Marilyn Harran

for the same reason that Jewish deportations generally were not—and here the Poles were not being deported to their extermination. The system of isolated ghettos established by the occupiers kept the Jews unaware of what was happening elsewhere and put them at the mercy of German violence. The premeditated and criminal brutality employed by the occupiers for the physical degradation of the population of the ghetto (involving extreme measures of starvation and exposure to epidemic, generating massive fatalities) weakened the Jewish will and the potential for resistance. The Germans also employed the principle of collective punishment, with iron consequences, causing anxiety among the ghetto population that any resistance would result in persecution on an even larger scale.

2) **The almost total isolation of the Jews:** Only those Poles who were unafraid of the threat of a death sentence for helping Jews and felt the need to save their neighbors—the exception rather than the rule among a population involved to a large degree with the problems of their own survival—hastened to save them.

3) **Lack of resources:** The vast majority of Jews had nowhere to go. Hiding outside of the ghetto was exceedingly difficult and dangerous. Most Jews simply did not have the necessary prerequisites:

a way to survive off the land, and facial features and accents that would not betray them. Rarely did someone want to take them in. There were known cases of Jews who managed to break out of ghettos and transit camps, only to be caught through the help of the surrounding population and, in the end, not escaping death. Attempts by Jews to establish their own partisan units or forest hideouts usually ended tragically because Polish villagers fed and protected "their" partisans, but treated groups of Jews who tried to acquire food as criminals. The feelings of separation and isolation gave rise to an atmosphere of resignation among most Jews.

Without acknowledging these realities, one cannot understand the condition of the Jews at that time. If one takes them into consideration, however, the amount of Jewish resistance—despite the reality that, in all the occupied countries, only a minority of the population defied the persecution—is astonishing.

FELIKS TYCH is a professor of modern history who specializes in the history of the Holocaust and director of the Jewish Historical Institute in Warsaw. He is the author of *Długi cień Zagłady. Szkice historyczne* (The Long Shadow of the Shoah), 2004, science editor and co-author of the book *Pamięć. Historia Żydów polskich przed, w czasie i po Zagładzie* (Remembrance. A History of Polish Jews before, during, and after the Shoah), and chief editor of the series "Archiwum Ringelbluma" (Ringelblum Archives), initiated in 1997.

MICHAEL BERENBAUM

▸ 13. Was the Holocaust inevitable?

The absence of vast governmental protest,
the lack of condemnation, and the failure to take
symbolic or real action on behalf of the victims
made it easier for the killers to kill the Jews and
to presume that the world acquiesced.

Let me try my hand at imagining ten ways that the Holocaust might never have happened:

I. If Adolf Hitler never came to power...

It is axiomatic to believe that no Hitler, no Holocaust; but the Holocaust required that *many* within German society and that *almost all* German social institutions share or acquiesce to Hitler's racist vision that divided the world according to race and that saw the Jews as a cancer on the German nation, whose salvation could only be achieved by the elimination of the Jews.

Hitler came to power before the Weimar democracy no longer commanded the allegiance of the nation, because the center had collapsed and the antidemocratic radical right and the radical left—Nazis and Communists—had a majority in the Reichstag.

II. If German public opinion had responded more vigorously to the assault against the Jews...

The initial acts against the Jews were testing the waters to see how far the German nation could be pushed, how deeply they could be brought around to support the policies of Hitler and the Nazis against the Jews; on April 7, 1933, Jews were expelled from the civil service, including teachers and professors as well as physicians. On May 10 of the same year, Hitler's 100th day in office, German students and their professors burned un-Germanic books, including books by Jewish authors, in bonfires in many cities within Germany. These were the early days of the regime. Had the public expressed its displeasure, the assault against the Jews might have been less extreme and the Nazis might have proceeded far more cautiously.

III. If other countries had been willing to receive the Jews...

The first goal of Nazi policies against the Jews was to force them to leave, to make their life within Germany difficult, if not impossible, and to show them that life would be better anywhere else.

←————————————————————————————————

Previous page: Passengers of the *SS St. Louis* looking toward the port of Havana. The *SS St. Louis* departed Hamburg for Havana in May 1937 with 937 Jewish refugees on board. After Cuba cancelled its agreement to admit the refugees, the ship headed for Florida. For two weeks the ship sailed along the coast of Florida, looking for asylum in the United States. When it failed to obtain asylum in June 1939, it returned to Europe, where France, Great Britain, Holland, and Belgium agreed to admit the passengers. With the German occupation of France, Holland, and Belgium, they shared the fate of all European Jews. Probably, most of them died. Courtesy of USHMM

Jewish family during the displacement from their home in Cracow, 1940-41.
Courtesy of the Jewish Historical Institute

Sadly, there were no countries willing to receive Jews in the numbers necessary to facilitate their removal from German soil. Hitler and his supporters assumed that no one wanted the Jews. Only they were willing to do something about it.

IV. If Germany had not been allowed to rearm...

The Versailles Treaty at the end of World War I placed strict limitations on the size and composition of the German army. The Nazis regarded that as a humiliation and made no secret of their desire to rearm. At several points during 1933-39, the West could have prevented a still weak Germany from rearming; it chose to do otherwise, and by the time it was forced to act, Germany was a world power that required all the might of the United States, the Soviet Union, Great Britain, and their Allies to defeat.

V. If the churches—Catholic and Protestant—within Germany and without, had spoken out...

The first killings were not of Jews; they were of mentally retarded and physically handicapped Germans who were considered "life unworthy of living," and were gassed in six "euthanasia centers" on Hitler's direct orders. Such killing was stopped when the parents of the victims and the Church leaders protested.

When the Jews were gassed, there was a deep silence from the Church, which in Germany had become allied with the Nazi regime or, at best, acquiescent to it. There was also a virtual silence from the Vatican.

VI. If, after June 1941, the German army as well as local gendarmerie and native anti-Semites had not cooperated in the killing of Jews by the Mobile Killing Units...

The killing of Jews began in June 1941 with the German invasion of the Soviet Union and Soviet-occupied territories. Joining the German Army were 3,000 troops that swept into towns, villages, and hamlets and murdered the local Jewish population. They did not act alone. The professional German army, which had a long military tradition against killing non-combatants, cooperated and participated in the killing of innocent civilians—women, children, and the elderly, not only men of combat age. And they were assisted by local anti-Semites and local police. It would have been impossible for so few to murder so many without the cooperation of these additional resources. Had more outsiders refused to participate—had they refused to cooperate or even to identify Jews—the numbers of Jews killed would have been much smaller.

VII. If more Germans had refused to kill Jews...

There was a widespread debate during the 1990s as to the motivations of the killers. However deep their disagreements, most scholars agree that there is no evidence that a person who refused to participate in genocide on the grounds of conscience was ever punished for his act.

In other words, the killers had a choice whether to participate. They might have lost face by refusing to kill; they might have been unpopular with the members of their unit, but they faced no harm if they just said no. Few—far too few—refused to slaughter the innocent.

VIII. If the Allies had protested more loudly, more boldly, more often, and more vehemently...

The absence of vast governmental protest, the lack of condemnation, and the failure to take symbolic or real action on behalf of the victims made it easier for the killers to kill the Jews and to presume that the world acquiesced.

One important student of this period said: "The Holocaust may have been unstoppable"— nothing that the Allies could have done may have been able to stop it—"but it should have been unbearable, and it wasn't."

Another keen observer said: "In the end the pessimists won. They said that nothing could be done and nothing was." We will never know if the optimists were right, that indeed something could have been done.

IX. If there had been more rescuers...

It took courage to offer to shelter a person for an indefinite time, even for a day and an hour, to risk one's safety and the safety of one's family. Had people been more decent and brave, there is no doubt that many fewer would have been killed, and many more saved.

X. If the killers had been less determined...

The murder of the Jews became the national obsession of the German people, and most especially of their leadership. The pace of killing intensified, even after everyone knew that the war was lost. The command to eliminate the Jews was an essential part of Hitler's last will and testament, and there were many times when a less focused, less obsessed group would have put an end to the process and done other things.

Notice that I have not written of the victims and what they could have done. First of all, I regard it as unfair to blame the victims for their own victimization. Secondly, more Jews would have left had there been places to go, and thirdly, resistance—armed uprising—was never a choice of how to live or whether to live, but a decision of what to do in the face of death, to acquiesce or to resist. The fighters were mostly young; they were responsible only for themselves, and not for young children whom they had to provide for or for elderly parents who depended on them. Most people could not think of themselves and of history alone. Many bore heavy burdens with as much dignity and decency as they could muster under impossible situations, facing choiceless choices.

MICHAEL BERENBAUM is a writer, lecturer, filmmaker, and teacher consulting in the conceptual development of museums. He is also an adjunct Professor of Theology at the University of Judaism in Los Angeles and director of its Sigi Ziering Institute: Exploring the Ethical and Religious Implications of the Holocaust. He was the project director of the United States Holocaust Memorial Museum. He is the author of numerous books such as *After Tragedy and Triumph, The World Must Know,* and *Anatomy of the Auschwitz Death Camp.*

Andrzej Paczkowski

▶ 14. Why were Jews murdered in Poland after the war?

Many were killed trying to return to their homes, only to realize they were occupied by someone else, and others were victimized for trying to reclaim their seized property. Still others were persecuted as the personification of the hated Communist government, even if they did not have anything to do with Communism. Nevertheless, their presence constituted a remorseful reminder of the war years, quietly recalling those dying in the ghettos, the transports, the columns of people marching to their deaths.

Funeral of the victims of the pogrom in Kielce at the Jewish cemetery in Kielce, July 1946. Courtesy of USHMM

Estimates of the number of Jews murdered in Poland during the years 1945-47 have varied from 800 to 1,500. After 1989, when historians gained unrestricted access to archives, no specific research on this phenomenon was undertaken, and so there is no way of telling which estimate is closer to the truth. No matter what the exact number, however, it is certain that on Polish soil in the first few years following World War II, murders of Jews were numerous. There were certainly more of them than in other countries of Central and Eastern Europe. More importantly and interestingly, there were more murders than during the interwar period, when many pogroms and other acts of aggression had taken place.

The causes for these incidents were multiple. It is difficult to discuss them all, but I will begin with the most important one.

In the period immediately following the war, anarchy and chaos reigned in many regions of the country. (Both marauders and Red Army soldiers played a role in this breakdown.) Attacks and thievery were a daily occurrence, and tens of thousands of people owned weapons and made use of them in disputes with their neighbors.

Previous page: Mourners and the local community at the common grave of victims of the pogrom in Kielce, July 1946. Courtesy of USHMM

Of course, this is not a sufficient explanation for why violence was directed at Jews. In Polish society there had existed for ages deep layers of anti-Semitism (and xenophobia, more generally), and anti-Jewish attitudes and reactions had intensified in the 1930s, particularly due to economic crisis and widespread anti-Semitic agitation. During the war, anti-Semitism not only did not weaken, but rather the opposite: It intensified and became more widespread. Within the territory incorporated into the Soviet Union, Poles became a "second-class" community, and they considered the beneficiaries of the new situation to be, above all, Jews (as well as Ukrainians, Byelorussians, and Lithuanians).

Under the German occupation, Nazi propaganda reinforced anti-Semitic stereotypes (among others, the revelation regarding the murders at Katyn) and, more significantly, the Germans encouraged the Poles to persecute Jews. They did so both directly, for example, rewarding those who turned in Jewish fugitives from the ghettos and camps, and indirectly, offering opportunities for Poles (as well as Ukrainians, Byelorussians and Lithuanians) to take possession of "Jewish property," permitting robbery and the occupation of homes, apartments, and shops. The seizure of Jewish homes and businesses mostly took place in smaller cities and towns, where Jews had been

Woman bewailing the death of her husband murdered during the pogrom in Kielce, July 1946. Courtesy of USHMM

a large, often the largest ethnic group. That Jews seemed about to disappear forever provided many Poles with the opportunity to benefit from stealing their property. How much was taken is impossible to estimate. Many (again, an unknown number) who followed their national and spiritual leaders took political or ideological satisfaction in the disappearance of the Jews, believing that a danger to the nation state had disappeared.

Then suddenly, along came the Red Army and its Communist government, and Jews were back again, both those who had survived the occupation (usually by being hidden by other Poles), and those who had come from the east. There appeared two common types of Jewish figures: the owners of recently seized (and often shabby) goods, and those holding positions at various levels of the government apparatus, including the coercive forces, the military, the press, and the governing party.

Postwar anti-Semitism, therefore, became a novelty that proved in some respects more ominous than in earlier times. One may reach this conclusion from the number of Jews who fell victim to violence during this time. Many were killed trying to return to their homes, only to realize they were occupied by someone else, and others were victimized for trying to reclaim their seized property or—as many were convinced —their own "unearthed" hidden valuables. Still others were persecuted as the personification of the hated Communist government, their servants or henchmen, even if they had nothing to do with Communism. Nevertheless, their very presence constituted a remorseful reminder of the war years, quietly recalling those dying of hunger in the ghettos, the transports, the columns of people marching to their deaths, and the fugitives who were hunted down.

ANDRZEJ PACZKOWSKI is a professor of history at the Institute of Political Studies in the Polish Academy of Sciences, professor at the Collegium Civitas. He is the author of numerous books, including *Prasa polska 1918-1939* (The Polish Press 1918-1939), 1980, *Stanisław Mikołajczyk, czyli klęska realisty* (Stanislaw Mikolajczyk, or the Failure of a Realist), 1991, *Pół wieku dziejów Polski* (A Half-Century of Polish History), 1995.

Andrzej Paczkowski

▶ 15. How many Jews were functionaries of the Security Service in the 1940s and 1950s?

In the years 1944-56, out of approximately fifty people who filled leadership positions in the Polish Ministry of Public Security, Jews made up 29 percent. This was a surprisingly high percentage. Most Jews were in the higher, more prominent positions, while the fewest number filled the lowest rungs of the hierarchy. Noticeably, more Jews were in the ministry than in its local operations. There were generally no Jews—a few at most—in the majority of district government offices.

In the years 1944-56, out of approximately fifty people who filled leadership positions in the Polish Ministry of Public Security, Jews made up 29 percent. This was a surprisingly high percentage, given the Jewish population in postwar Poland, and had two basic causes:

1) As of 1944, the Communist Party—at first a hegemonic power and from 1948 holding a monopoly of power in Poland—assigned important state posts to trusted individuals. Among these were primarily people who before 1930 had been members of the Communist Party or its youth affiliates. The security apparatus found itself under special constraints, as it played a key role in the process of achieving and preserving power, and in building the foundations of the totalitarian state; thus many prewar Communists and Communist sympathizers were employed in its creation.

2) Considering the ethnic structure of interwar Poland, and the reluctant and often hostile relations among the political powers, (as well as the relation of the Polish state to its ethnic minorities who made up about one third of the population), the Communist movement, given its complete revision of the form and character of the nation, seemed particularly attractive to Jews, Byelorussians, and Ukrainians. As a result, in many regions and professional environments, Jews made up the majority or the largest ethnic group among party members.

Some authors and historians believe that Jozef Stalin's own politics played a role in imposing an overrepresentation of Jews in executive positions. It was his way of ensuring that the governing Communists were cut off from the majority population, while at the same time remaining completely dependent upon his favor. Until today, however, no single document has been found to support this theory. Indeed, the opposite was true: In reports sent to Moscow by Soviet advisors and the Soviet embassy in Warsaw, attention was repeatedly drawn to the problem of Jewish overrepresentation in the Polish security appara-

---

Previous page: Propaganda poster showing Jozef Stalin and Boleslaw Bierut, president of the Republic of Poland, from the Polish People's Republic period. Photo by M. Nehring

May Day mass meeting at Plac Zwyciestwa, with Boleslaw Bierut, the president of the Republic of Poland, surrounded by the members of the government. Second from the left is Jakub Berman, responsible for the Ministry of Public Security, Warsaw, 1949. Photo by W. Kondracki/PAP

tus. This tendency had already been manifest in 1945-46, but became particularly clear in 1948-49, when the Soviet Union initiated its own anti-Semitic campaign.

Nevertheless, the presence of Jews in the security apparatus could be described as taking the form of an "inverted pyramid" rather than an "iceberg." Most Jews were in the higher, more prominent positions, while the fewest number filled the lowest rungs of the hierarchy. Noticeably, more Jews were in the ministry than in its local operations. There were generally no Jews—a few at most—in the majority of district government offices. In December 1945, when the Security Service numbered more than 22,000 employees, there were about 500 Jews among them, making up only 2.5 percent, and this percentage diminished as the security apparatus grew to 33,000 in 1953. The problem, therefore, lay in the fact that people of Jewish ancestry were concentrated in the key posts: vice-ministers, department directors, division managers, and chiefs of *voievodeship* (local administrative councils) services. This problem was already present during the period of the creation of the Security Service, whereas later on a mechanism functioned to attract as employees people trusted by those already in positions of responsibility because of their shared political activities or prison time.

The concentration of Jews in leadership positions—which, in reality, included the party apparatus, the press, the political apparatus and the military, and the staff of economic departments—aroused objection among several leading party functionaries. For example, in a letter to Stalin in 1948, Wladyslaw Gomulka (then first secretary of the Polish Communist Party) tried to reduce the number of Jews in the party, but his colleagues in the party leadership opposed him, though there were those who backed him, particularly among Security Service functionaries. Gomulka's stance stemmed mainly from the fear that this situation would hinder the Communists from gaining legitimacy, would deepen anti-Communist sentiments and thus anti-state sentiments in Polish society, and would propagate the stereotype of "Jewish Communism."

Despite Stalin's anti-Semitic politics, in Poland the situation never came to anti-Semitic purges, neither in the security apparatus nor in other sectors of the government. Only in 1956, amid the wave of condemnations of "mistakes and distortions," were the majority of Jews removed from the security apparatus, and the last left in 1968, during a general government-led anti-Semitic campaign. But the situation that had existed in 1944-56 solidified the conviction among many Poles that it was precisely the Jews who were, above all, responsible for the crimes of Stalinism.

ANDRZEJ PACZKOWSKI is a professor of history at the Institute of Political Studies in the Polish Academy of Sciences, and professor at the Collegium Civitas. He is the author of numerous books, including *Prasa polska 1918-1939* (The Polish Press 1918-1939), 1980, *Stanisław Mikolajczyk, czyli klęska realisty* (Stanislaw Mikolajczyk, or the Failure of a Realist), 1991, and *Pół wieku dziejów Polski* (A Half-Century of Polish History), 1995.

Dariusz Stola

▶ 16. Why were Jews thrown out of Poland in 1968?

In the spring of 1968, a strident, aggressive campaign against "Zionists" swept through Poland. "Anti-Zionism" was a camouflage for an operation that was directed, in practice, against Jews in general, Poles of Jewish ancestry, and even people who had nothing to do with anything Jewish.

In the spring of 1968, a strident, aggressive campaign against "Zionists" swept through Poland. "Anti-Zionism" was a camouflage for an operation that was directed, in practice, against Jews in general, Poles of Jewish ancestry, and even people who had nothing to do with anything Jewish. In this campaign of hatred, known as the "March events" (because it began in March 1968), Jews were not the only target of attacks, but they were the first and the intended one. The campaign was initiated by what was then the government of Poland and was carried out using time-tested schemes of action from earlier hate campaigns in Poland and other Communist countries.

In the course of the campaign, the government announced that those "who recognize Israel as their fatherland" could leave Poland. They needed only file an application agreeing to leave and renouncing their Polish citizenship. On this basis, in the years 1968-71 nearly 13,000 people left Poland, of whom only a minority managed to make it to Israel. Given that on the eve of March 1968 approximately 25,000 Jews lived in Poland, one can say that more than half the Jews left.

In a country where every year tens of thousands of people were declined permission to travel abroad, opening the doors for the "Zionists" was presented as a gesture of good will. In this way, the Communist system showed its hypocrisy, not only in that it publicized lies, but because it made its citizens participate in a grotesque charade in which the meanings of words and actions were distorted. According to this logic, the government actually didn't "throw the Jews out" of Poland, but rather "accommodated" them, while "incentives" were offered (read: pressure and threats) to those who hesitated. It was precisely this overwhelming, unbearable atmosphere of the "anti-Zionist" campaign that was the main factor pushing Jews to emigrate; it was characterized by their defenselessness against attacks, feelings of rejection and alienation, and an awakening of their own bad memories and anxieties, as well as those regarding their loved ones.

What did the March campaign consist of? It was based, in the first place, on a propaganda campaign—a wave of aggressive, slanderous statements in the press, radio, and television. In it, "Zionists" were accused of intending to overthrow the government and of committing

←───

Previous page: Demonstration with anti-Semitic slogans, Warsaw, 1968.
Courtesy of the Institute of Political Studies of the Polish Academy of Sciences

crimes, in the Stalinist era, of corruption, cronyism, and abuse, of maligning Poland and Poles around the world, and even of collaboration with the Germans during the war. The accusations were often simply absurd—indeed, the power of slander does not lie in the strength of its arguments—and wretched, aggressive propaganda was put forth everywhere. Practically all newspapers, radio stations, and television channels were controlled by the party, and journalists and editors typically adhered zealously to the guidelines coming down from above; many even attacked Jews out of their own commitment and honest enthusiasm.

The second current of the campaign consisted of mass rallies and meetings—the largest of which drew up to 100,000 people—although the thousands of smaller gatherings organized at workplaces by local party committees, professional associations, youth organizations, etc., had a greater impact. Millions of people took part in these, listening to aggressive speeches, carrying banners with "anti-Zionist" slogans, and raising their hands to such resolutions. They did so out of a habit of obedience, as well as out of opportunism and fear, but not infre-

Poles of Jewish descent emigrating after the events of 1968.
Photo by Z. Siemaszko/Forum

Luggage of Jews emigrating from Poland to Israel after the events of March 1968. Photo by Z. Siemaszko/Forum

quently also with the conviction that the government was right, that Jews were the enemy of Poland, or Stalinists, or a privileged caste. Anti-Jewish slogans found fertile ground in old, deeply rooted biases.

The third current of the campaign was a purge—the removal of "Zionists" from their positions in the party, at work, or at school—often carried out along with public humiliation and indignity. To this was added various kinds of harassment by the Security Service, zealous party activists, or simply envious professional colleagues or suspicious neighbors. The campaign gave carte blanche to the activities of careerists and opportunists, mudslingers and informants who were encouraged to vileness in the settling of private scores.

Why did the government unleash this campaign? It began a few days after the outbreak of student protests in Warsaw, which spread to many cities across the country. The government responded with brutal attacks by police and party activists armed with truncheons. "Anti-Zionist" propaganda was meant to convince society that the rebellion was inspired by a small but influential group of young people coming from the families of Jewish party activists. It was precisely these

Jewish Communists—who the day before had held high positions in the state and now wanted to return to power—who were supposed to be the hidden engines of the unrest. They were presented as part of a larger anti-Polish conspiracy aligned with influential Jewish organizations in the West, the West German government, and the CIA. This entire plot was clearly the manifestation of a paranoid "conspiracy theory" that awakened fear and hatred among Poles toward these alleged enemies of their country.

The government kindled anti-Jewish resentments out of fear that youth from across the social spectrum would join the revolt. These fears were strengthened by the fact that in neighboring Czechoslovakia there had arisen precisely this sort of powerful movement on behalf of systemic reform, which Wladyslaw Gomulka and other leaders of the PRL (Polish People's Republic) labeled a "counterrevolution." Secondly, Jews were made the scapegoats, burdened with the guilt for the absurdities and injustices of the system. Thirdly, a battle with "Zionists" was also looked upon favorably in Moscow, which supported the Arabs against the Israelis in the Middle East conflict. And finally, behind the scenes, the March events also enabled an old score, internal to the PZPR (Polish United Workers' Party), to be settled. There had been a battle of party factions in which the leading role had been played by supporters of General Mieczyslaw Moczar, chief of the Ministry of Domestic Affairs, who had skillfully manipulated his subordinates in the Secret Service. Among these subordinates it was particularly common to encounter anti-Jewish prejudices or even outright obsessions. Their political interests played easily into their hateful convictions.

DARIUSZ STOLA is a historian at the Institute of Political Studies in the Polish Academy of Sciences, as well as professor and deputy president at the Collegium Civitas.

today

Memory and Knowledge about the Holocaust

ROBERT SZUCHTA AND PIOTR TROJANSKI

▶ 17. What is taught about the Holocaust in Polish schools today?

Due to logistical considerations and the desire to hide their crimes from their own people and from the world, the Nazis chose to locate their main ghettos, concentration camps, and extermination camps within occupied Poland. The greatest drama of World War II took place here, against the will of the Poles, but in their presence. Therefore, this crime is an important part not only of Jewish, European, and world history, but also of Polish history.

Recent educational reforms in Poland allow history teachers to choose freely both a curriculum and a textbook to be used. It is thus up to the teachers to decide how much time and attention they will devote to the subject of Jewish culture and history in Poland, as well as to the Holocaust. There are textbooks that reference these issues only generally, but others, such as the one we wrote, *The Holocaust: To Understand Why*, go into greater detail.

Our textbook on the Holocaust teaches about the planned, institutionally organized, and systematically executed extermination of six million European Jews during the years of World War II. These exceptional crimes were committed by the German Nazis and their helpers. As the site of the extermination, they chose the occupied territory of Eastern Europe, where the largest concentration of Jews lived. Due to logistical considerations—that is, the need to minimize transportation costs—and the desire to hide their crimes from their own people and from the world, they chose to locate their main ghettos, concentration camps, and extermination camps within occupied Poland. The greatest drama of World War II took place here, against the will of the Poles, but in their presence. Therefore, this crime is an important part not only of Jewish, European, and world history, but also of Polish history.

All Polish students, from ages nine to eighteen, take history classes about World War II. They learn about the origins of the criminal Nazi ideology, the reasons for the establishment of the Third Reich in Germany, and the role of Adolf Hitler and his closest collaborators in planning and carrying out the Holocaust. They discuss the problems of anti-Semitism and racism in Germany, and consider their negative effects, past and present. Next they familiarize themselves with the causes and the course of World War II, and the situation of Polish citizens under the German and Soviet occupations, taking note of the particularly tragic fate of the Jewish nation. In studying the next phase of the war, they analyze the successive stages of the Holocaust: the loss of public rights for Jews in Germany in 1935, the anti-Jewish pogrom of 1938 called *Kristallnacht*, the Nazi plans for a "final solution to the Jewish question," later carried out by the Germans in occupied Poland.

Previous page: Lesson about the Holocaust in a high school in Warsaw, "Oswiecim = crime, pain," January 14, 2005. Photo by M. Grzelak/Forum

The Grodzka Gate-NN Theater, a municipal institution of culture housed in Lublin's Old Town, organized a program for young Poles to write letters to a nine-year-old Jewish boy, Henio Zytomirski, who was killed in Majdanek death camp. Thus young people honored the Polish Day of Memory of the Holocaust.
Photo by M. Trembecki/PAP

An important phase of the Holocaust, discussed in detail during history classes, is the establishment of ghettos by the Germans. Students discover that the ghettos were an indirect means of exterminating the Jews. They learn about the lives of the ghetto inhabitants and the organization of their government, cultural, communal, political, and youth institutions. Important themes discussed in class include the situation of the Jews and their relations with Poles in the eastern territories of Poland occupied by the USSR during 1939-41, and the genocidal activities of the *Einsatzgruppen* after the start of the war with Russia in June of 1941.

Students learn about the crucial phase of the Holocaust that took place in Nazi extermination camps in occupied Poland. The names of Auschwitz-Birkenau, Treblinka, Belzec, Sobibor, Majdanek, Chelmno, and Sztutowo (Stutthof) are familiar to the students. They know about gas chambers, "special treatment," *Sonderkommando*, "special actions," deportation, and other euphemisms used by the Nazis to hide their crimes. They learn that the Auschwitz camp in the town of Oswiecim was established in 1940 by the Germans as a criminal concentration camp for Poles, and later, as Auschwitz-Birkenau, became an extermination camp for one million European Jews. Today Auschwitz-Birkenau is a symbol of the Holocaust.

Another theme is the Jewish civil and military resistance movement in the ghettos, concentration camps, and extermination camps, and the activities of Jewish partisan units. Much space is devoted to examination of the Warsaw Ghetto uprising of 1943. Students know of the military resistance of Mordecai Anielewicz and Marek Edelman as well as the passive resistance of Janusz Korczak and Emanuel Ringelblum. They know that the uprising was the first attempted armed resistance in German-occupied Europe, and that it was organized by youthful combatants of the Jewish Fighting Organization.

Polish students also learn about the postwar fate of the few Jews fortunate enough to avoid the extermination, thanks in part to the heroism of Poles. They study the pogrom in Kielce in 1946, the anti-Semitic campaign of 1968 in Poland, and the establishment of the State of Israel in its past and present circumstances.

As preparation for studying the Holocaust, students familiarize themselves with the most important events in the centuries-old his-

School lesson at the Auschwitz-Birkenau State Museum.
Courtesy of the Auschwitz-Birkenau State Museum in Oswiecim

tory and culture of European Jewry. They learn that in medieval times Jews were persecuted because of their religion; that, escaping from Western European persecution, they found safety on Polish lands, which, as a "Republic of Many Nations," was for centuries their second fatherland, "Polin." In this context, they study the religious tolerance that prevailed in old Poland and the shared experiences of Poles and Jews in the fourteenth century. Regarding the nineteenth and the beginning of the twentieth centuries, they do not avoid such challenging themes as the growing anti-Semitism among Poles, which often led to conflicts between the two communities.

The interwar period is presented to Polish students, on the one hand, as an unprecedented time of flowering of Jewish communal, cultural, and economic life in the Second Republic, but on the other hand, as a period of increasing anti-Semitism, triggered by the difficult economic situation of the country and the events in Nazi Germany. Acknowledging both the bright spots and the shadows of Polish-Jewish life before World War II allows students to encounter the praiseworthy pages of their own history—such as the mission of Jan Karski to inform the Free World about the Holocaust; efforts to save and help Jews, and the sympathy for murdered Jews (Irena Sendlerowa, Henryk Slawik)—but also the dark ones, such as Polish complicity in the crimes at Jedwabne on July 10, 1941, or Polish extortion or blackmailing of Jews. For the most part, these are new themes for students, and the truths revealed by Polish historians are frequently difficult for society as a whole to accept. Therefore, it is not easy to study these issues.

In conclusion, we would stress that, since 2003, Polish students have been using a primary textbook to study the Holocaust, and the teachers are given a detailed curriculum on how to present this issue. Study trips to sites of former concentration and extermination camps are systematically organized; there young people encounter the history surrounding these memorials, as well as what happened there, in an atmosphere of immediacy. Museums also play a role in teaching about the Holocaust in Poland, as exhibitions on this topic often take place. Some exhibitions such as "Anne Frank—a History for Today" or "Jews in Poland: Our Own, or Foreigners?" are shown in schools, giving students the opportunity for direct contact with Holocaust history. Opportunities are created for students to exchange knowledge on this topic through a variety of competitions organized across Poland. Internet access also plays a significant role, as students find web pages dedicated to scholarship on Holocaust history and the history of the Jews.

ROBERT SZUCHTA is a historian and a high school teacher in Warsaw, who initiated contacts between the Polish and Israeli school systems. He is co-author of *The Holocaust: To Understand Why*, the first Polish textbook on the Holocaust.

DR. PIOTR TROJANSKI is a historian at the Institute of History of the Pedagogical Academy in Cracow. He is co-author of *The Holocaust: To Understand Why*, the first Polish textbook on the Holocaust.

ANNA BIKONT

▶ 18. How much do Poles know about the anti-Semitic excesses that occurred during World War II?

During the heated debates that took place in 2001 surrounding the Jedwabne affair, one question arose again and again: How was it possible that crimes of this scale went unexposed for sixty years? And yet it is precisely this point that is unexceptional. The entire historical record, not only Polish-Jewish relations, was falsified during the Communist era.

Poles know about Jedwabne—the small town in eastern Poland, where on July 10, 1941, Polish townspeople burned their Jewish neighbors to death in a barn. The catalyst for this public revelation was the book *Neighbors* by Jan Gross, a professor of sociology at New York University, who put forth a dramatic thesis: It was no band of hooligans that corralled their Jewish neighbors and burnt them alive—men, women, and children, tossed onto the blistering flames—but rather the crime had been committed by ordinary Polish citizens. The decisive moment in what has come to be known as "the Jedwabne affair" was the declaration by Polish president Aleksander Kwasniewski that he intended to publicly apologize for the deeds of his co-nationals, and he called for a penitential mass to be conducted by Polish bishops. The Institute of National Memory began an investigation that resulted in the determination that "the perpetrators of the crimes, in a strict sense, were Polish townspeople."

During the heated debates that took place in 2001 surrounding the Jedwabne affair, one question arose again and again: How was it possible that crimes of this scale went unexposed for sixty years? And yet it is precisely this point that is unexceptional. The entire historical record, not only Polish-Jewish relations, was falsified during the Communist era. History during these years meant Marxist history, which knew only about, on one side, the exploiters—landowners and the bourgeoisie and on the other, the working class and peasants. "Jews" had no place in this version of history. They appeared suddenly—from where we do not know—during the war, only to be murdered in the camps. Their absence from "official discourse" in Marxist theory furthered the process of their disappearance from history.

Poles, who had themselves suffered immensely during the war, did not want to remember that they were living on top of a giant Jewish cemetery, nor that the houses in which they lived belonged a short time ago to their Jewish neighbors. "On the day after the murder not a single Jewish home stood empty," I was told by a witness of the Jedwabne crimes. Afterwards, it was simply not discussed. It happened, period.

Previous page: Monument commemorating the mass murder of the Jews of Jedwabne in July 1941, at the hands of Poles, with the inscription: "In memory of the Jews of Jedwabne and surrounding areas, men, women, and children, fellow dwellers of this land, murdered and burned alive at this site on 10 July, 1941. Jedwabne, July 10, 2001." Photo by A. Kardasz/PAP

 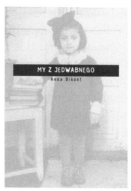 

Publications related to the mass murder in Jedwabne: Anna Bikont's
My, z Jedwabnego (We, People from Jedwabne), Jan Tomasz Gross's *Sąsiedzi* (Neighbors),
and *Wokół Jedwabnego* (Around Jedwabne), edited by Paweł Machcewicz and Krzysztof
Persak.

This same silence fell over the entire country after the war. Poles had
watched as genocidal crimes were committed before their eyes—crimes
they could not prevent, and in the face of which few of them had offered help. They too had been victims of the horrors of the war. Yet after the war they could have mourned for the nation that had perished
on their soil—but they did not. Their Jewish fellow-citizens, who had
lived here for centuries, were remembered only in whispers and mutter-
ings. Even today in guidebooks to small Polish towns where the majority of inhabitants had been Jewish, one often finds not a single word
acknowledging their presence—or absence.

For several months the Jedwabne affair remained fixed in the headlines of newspapers and television news shows. Jedwabne was discussed
in shops and on the streetcar. Thanks to the exposure of the crimes, an
opportunity arose for the present generation to do what their parents
had never done: Mourn for the dead, seek out their traces, appreciate the
contributions of assimilated Jews to Polish culture, and value the distinctiveness of those Jews for whom assimilation had not been a goal.

It was not, unfortunately, only in Jedwabne that genocide took place.
Five days prior to the Jedwabne incident, from the night of July 5 until
July 6, 1941, Polish inhabitants of the nearby town of Wasosz used axes,
poles, and pitchforks to murder their Jewish neighbors. On July 7 the
Polish villagers of Radzilow, also not far from Jedwabne, set fire to their
fellow Jewish villagers in a barn. In some two hundred locations, during

that period and in that area—a swath of northeastern Poland—smaller and larger pogroms took place. Some occurred even before the Germans invaded the villages that the Soviet army had abandoned. These events did not have the same impact on Polish public consciousness as Jedwabne did, but they were exposed and recorded by historians of the Institute of National Memory.

Over all, very little is known about the scale of anti-Jewish excesses perpetrated by Poles. But in the course of the next few years, or at most the next few decades, we will likely witness an accounting of these deeds. Since 1989, many young historians have taken as their task the investigation of Polish-Jewish relations during World War II. In the wake of the Jedwabne affair, new historians have emerged. What they find will come as a painful shock.

ANNA BIKONT is a *Gazeta Wyborcza* journalist and writer. Together with Joanna Szczesna, she wrote a biography of Wislawa Szymborska. She is also the author of an album, *I ciągle widzę ich twarze. Fotografie polskich Żydów* (And I Still See Their Faces: The Photos of Polish Jews), and a book, *My, z Jedwabnego* (We, People from Jedwabne), 2004, in which she reconstructed the crimes committed against the Jewish inhabitants of Jedwabne and nearby Radzilow in July 1941 and decribed the fates of the would-be victims, murderers, witnesses, and righteous persons who, despite the local communities, hid and saved Jews.

YARON KAROL BECKER AND ALEX DANZIG

▸ 19. What are Israeli pupils taught about the Holocaust and World War II, and how?

In Israel a great deal of educational effort has been put on the content and methodology of teaching about and preserving memory of the Holocaust. Aside from lessons about Judaism, the Holocaust is the main theme that forms the national identity of young Israelis.

Israeli pupils are introduced in depth to the theme of the Holocaust and World War II in their second year of high school, in classes on the history of the Jewish nation. Until then, they have encountered the theme through school observances commemorating the Holocaust. Witnesses who personally survived and can testify to the events of that time are invited to the youngest primary school classes. On Israel's Holocaust Commemoration Day, there are many documentary programs about the Holocaust on television, and young people are encouraged to meet with the authors who write about the topic. Such readings, however, are not obligatory.

Study trips to Poland play an important role in Holocaust education. A portion of eleventh-grade pupils travel to Poland for eight to eleven days and visit sites of Jewish martyrology and Jewish resistance against the German occupiers. This is the main theme of such trips. Pupils are also introduced to the history and culture of Polish Jews and have an opportunity to encounter aspects of Polish culture and history as well. Participants in such trips take part in a special thirty-hour educational program during which they receive information pertaining to the subject. Approximately twenty-four to twenty-six class hours are devoted to presenting Jewish history and the Holocaust. The remaining hours are used to review the historical background of the Holocaust—that is, World War II and the general situation of Poland under German occupation. This is clearly too little to familiarize young people satisfactorily with the history of the war and the circumstances of the Holocaust. Their knowledge of this topic is thus fragmentary and insufficient.

The problematics of the Holocaust are presented to a significantly larger extent during the twelfth grade, just before graduation examinations. An effective curriculum is considered to contain approximately fifty class sessions about the Holocaust at this level of schooling, including ten hours dedicated to general issues concerning World War II.

The cycle of lessons about the Holocaust begins with a review of the phenomenon of increasing racism and anti-Semitism in Europe and throughout the world during the interwar period. The central object of study at this point is Germany after Hitler's rise to power. Much attention is paid to the Nuremberg laws and the Nazis' racist ideology. Pupils learn about the ideology of Aryan racial purity and how this ide-

---

Previous page: Young Israelis paying tribute to the victims of the Warsaw Ghetto. Photo by B. Zając

Lesson on the Holocaust in Israeli school. Courtesy of the Yad Vashem Institute

ology was incorporated into daily life. They study the genesis and course of the state-sponsored pogrom of *Kristallnacht* on November 9, 1938. The increasing anti-Semitism in Eastern Europe is also discussed, including the situation in Poland, Romania, and Hungary. Next they study the beginning of World War II, including the German aggression against Poland on September 1, 1939. The early persecution of Jews, including the establishment of the ghettos, is presented against the backdrop of the conditions of the occupation of Poland. Much attention is given to the conditions that existed in the ghetto, including the mere fight for survival—what we call "silent heroism."

The subsequent block of issues concerns the extermination of Jews in death camps and the Jewish reaction to their fate. The Jewish resistance movement is broadly discussed—the uprisings and armed resistance in the ghettos, the formation of Jewish partisan groups, and acts of resistance in the extermination camps. Directly after this, the postwar emigration of Jews to *Eretz Israel* (Palestine) is addressed, along with the rebirth of the Jewish nation after the war as an independent state.

It is necessary to emphasize that in Israel a great deal of educational effort has been put on the content and methodology of teaching about and preserving memory of the Holocaust. Aside from lessons about Judaism, the Holocaust is the main theme that forms the national identity of young Israelis. In Israel there are twelve centers for Holocaust education, primary among them being Yad Vashem. Israeli school pupils visit these centers regularly and participate in lessons and multi-day courses prepared for them. Despite continual improvement in the forms and methods of transmitting knowledge about the Holocaust, the issue of teaching about these tragic events, and especially the thematic range, provokes ongoing discussion involving all of Israeli society.

The general background of the Holocaust, or the history of World War II, is not sufficiently presented. For example, the battles on the Eastern Front are discussed in a very abbreviated fashion, and the defensive war in Poland in September 1939, if it is discussed at all, is highly abridged and typically cast in an entirely negative light. The Warsaw Uprising of August 1944 is not mentioned, and the majority of pupils are thus not aware that such an uprising ever broke out. As a result of recent open discussion in the Israeli media regarding teaching of the Holocaust, information about the extermination of Gypsies and the suffering of other nations during World War II, including the Poles, was introduced into the program of study. Nevertheless, there is still too little discussion of this theme.

Young people from Israel praying for the victims of the Auschwitz-Birkenau concentration camp, during the March of the Living. Photo by P. Turecki

Simultaneously, the emphasis is on the specificity of the Holocaust as a unique event, incomparable to any other, the next step in a direct lineage from ancient anti-Semitism and the anti-Semitism of the Christian Church, particularly during the Middle Ages. In this context, German Nazism is seen as simply a contemporary mutation of one eternal phenomenon of anti-Semitism. Such emphasis on the exclusivity of the Jewish Holocaust inhibits a consideration of the Holocaust in universal terms.

The formation of Holocaust memory in Israel—in which schools play a central role—reflects the process of Israeli national identity formation. It proceeds in a series of stages. Immediately after the war, there was relatively little discussion of Jewish martyrology. It was considered a painful, humiliating subject. In school it was rather heroism that was emphasized, exemplified in the theme of Jewish resistance, with the Warsaw Ghetto Uprising playing a central role. Only the heroic stance was valued. Victims of the Holocaust were looked down upon as sheep who were led to the slaughter. The *Judenrate* (Jewish councils) were judged in exclusively negative terms, with the activities of their members described as collaboration.

Just after the war, it was incredibly difficult for the survivors to tell their stories, not only because the truth was so horrible, but also because many people in Israel did not really want to hear them. Only after Adolf Eichmann's trial in 1961 was a flood of memories released, resulting in the entire nation turning a less raw, more sympathetic gaze upon its tragic past. Empathy for victims of the Holocaust enabled an understanding of the dramatic and tragic dilemmas they had been forced to confront. During this period the Holocaust became an obligatory topic of study in Israeli schools. It had been taught earlier, but after the Eichmann trial, a need was felt to treat the theme more systematically. It was also necessary to respond to the growing interest in the topic, to which American and European television films about the Holocaust had contributed greatly. Despite the typical superficiality of these stories—and often the artificial melodrama—they enabled our youth to identify with figures from the Holocaust era. Previously, it had been difficult for them to do so because they had been constrained by the use mainly of documents containing historical facts—without being exposed to emotional material that could cause them to feel estranged or traumatized. Subsequently, the process of teaching the Holocaust was based instead on the personal experiences of individuals who died or survived. They were no longer abstractions, but rather figures whose fates students could identify with.

In the past decade, during which there has been a great deal of Jewish emigration from the former USSR, including many people who had personal experiences of the war, more attention has been paid to the background of the war, and particularly its trajectory in Eastern Europe. Also, May 9 was designated in Israel as the Day of National Memory. Another factor that has intensified interest in the Holocaust among young people, and among Israelis in general, has been the increasing external threat to the nation. This has been the case with each successive war with Israel's neighbors, after which Israelis have felt themselves on the threshold of extermination.

For many years the study of the Holocaust was, in large part, isolated from the martyrology of other nations. Recently, that tendency is undergoing change. The program of historical study in junior high and high schools is constantly being reformed. Other victims of Nazi genocide are discussed within its framework. The content of school textbooks is being changed. Increasingly, they include discussions of the Righteous Among the Nations.

At present, the perspectives of teachers, parents, and Israeli society in general on the study of the Holocaust are very diverse. They depend on one's general worldview, and fluctuate between an extreme religionationalist attitude, in which there is no room for the victims and suffering of other nations, to a very liberal and humanistic attitude, which is more sensitive to every sacrifice. It could be said that in Israeli society there is a growing consciousness that education against racism and anti-Semitism is only possible if the message of the Holocaust is given universal meaning, which demands listening attentively to the suffering of other nations during World War II, as well as thereafter. And Israeli youth are beginning to sense that need, and to understand.

YARON KAROL BECKER, brought up in Poland, is a philosopher, journalist, and university lecturer who works at the Polish Institute in Tel Aviv.

ALEX DANZIG is a historian of Polish origin who lectures for tourist guides at the Yad Vashem Institute. He lives in Kibbutz Nir-Oz in the Negev Desert, and has the role of the main subject in the documentary films *Kibbutznik from Nir-Oz* and *Reading Sienkiewicz in the Negev Desert*.

Krystyna Oleksy

▶ 20. Do Poles visit the sites of Jewish extermination camps and what are their feelings when they do?

Poles—though not in great numbers—visit the sites of Jewish extermination camps. This is not a mass phenomenon, because the regions where the camps are located, with the exception of Majdanek,are not visited by large numbers of people, as they are far from significant cities and reaching them can be complicated. Despite this— with the exception of Treblinka—Polish visitors significantly outnumber those from abroad.

The answer to this question is sometimes oversimplified and narrowed to its first half: One then gets the impression that Poles do not visit these places because they do not care and have never cared about the extermination of Jews. However, the problem is more complicated, particularly in relation to the second half of the question, as it requires a description of the feelings of Polish visitors.

I think it would be useful if I begin by citing some statistics. With the exception of the Auschwitz-Birkenau museum, where quite precise statistics on visitation have been kept for many years, only very general data are available. We know, for example, that during the last three years, museums and memorial sites at Nazi camps of Jewish mass extermination were visited by the following approximate numbers:

Treblinka:

2003: 32,000 people, including 12,000 Poles
2004: 34,000 people, including 12,500 Poles
2005: 43,000 people, including 25,000 Poles

Polish visitors have included school groups above elementary level from the surrounding areas, as well as students from the teachers college, the graduating classes of nearby schools, and scouts from Warsaw. A significant group of Catholic youth who visit Cardinal Stefan Wyszynski's birthplace also found themselves in the area. For them, Treblinka was not the primary destination of their trip, but a visit occurred simply because it was "on the way."

Sobibor:

2003: 10,000 people, including 8,400 Poles
2004: 10,355 people, including more than 8,000 Poles
2005: 15,000 people, 85-90 percent of whom were Poles

The largest group of Polish visitors was made up of school groups from the Lublin area—both junior high and high school—as well as youth from Warsaw. Most of these visit a synagogue in Wlodawa be-

---

Previous page: Poles visiting the death camp in Belzec. Courtesy of the Auschwitz-Birkenau State Museum in Oswiecim

Poles visiting the death camp in Auschwitz-Birkenau. Courtesy of the Auschwitz-Birkenau State Museum in Oswiecim

fore their trip to Sobibor, to familiarize themselves with Jewish culture and tradition.

Majdanek:

2003: 85,000 people, including 50,000 Poles
2004: 100,000 people, including 50,000 Poles
2005: 122,000 people, including 76,000 Poles

The notably larger number of visitors to the Majdanek museum is correlated to the fact that it is located in a large university town situated in a thickly populated area.

Belzec:

Since its opening in June 2004, more than 30,000 people have visited, 96 percent of whom were Poles.

2005: 32,000 people, including 27,000 Poles

A significant proportion of the visitors are pupils from junior high and high schools, but many adults also visit. On Saturday and

Sunday individual visitors predominate; on these days they number up to 1,000 per day.

As the above data show, Poles—though not in great numbers—visit the sites of Jewish extermination camps. This is not a mass phenomenon because the regions where the camps are located, with the exception of Majdanek, are not visited by large numbers of people, as they are far from significant cities and reaching them can be complicated. Despite this—with the exception of Treblinka—Polish visitors significantly outnumber those from abroad.

Auschwitz

The number of visitors here far surpasses all other memorial sites:
2003: 480,000 people, including 200,000 Poles
2004: 580,000, including 200,000 Poles
2005: 900,000, including 330,000 Poles.

The Auschwitz museum is, to date, the only camp site where multiple studies of visitors have been carried out. These are aimed at gaining credible data on the level of knowledge of Polish pupils (from junior high and third-year high school classes) who visit the museum in large groups. Our researchers are also interested in understanding the motivations and problems of Polish teachers in preparing pupils to visit the camp sites, as well as the expectations of both groups concerning these visits. For example, how willing are teachers to call these trips "pilgrimages" to Auschwitz?

The answers given to questions regarding the ethnicity of camp victims testify that the knowledge that Jews made up the majority is widespread among Polish youth, regardless of whether the group involved was junior high or high school students. At the same time, they are aware of the Polish victims of the camp.

One theme of the researchers concerned the symbolism of Auschwitz. Young people understood it most often as a "universal" and "international" symbol—for them Auschwitz is "a place of genocide and extermination of mankind," a "place of suffering of people from many nations," or "a place of the extermination of Poles and Jews."

<hr>

Previous page: Children running to the gate of the camp in Auschwitz-Birkenau. SV/Forum

Much more difficult to measure is the question of how Poles feel during and after their visits. Here are a few comments made by visitors who filled out surveys or took part in discussion groups in their schools a few days after their visits to Auschwitz:

The visit to Auschwitz was for me an enormous experience. I was there for the first time, but that was enough for me to be able to imagine what happened there. It seemed to me that this camp was the largest massacre of people in all of Europe. I imagine how cruel the Germans were to the Jews. I learned many things relating to the camp.

I was afraid that this history could be repeated in the future. Fear of what happened. The visit to Auschwitz was something new and interesting for me, and at the same time terrifying. I learned how many people died in the camp and what the Germans did with the Jews: how they tortured them and what was left of them after. I still can't understand why the Germans murdered so many people and especially Jews. Because they were not guilty of anything.

For me what I experienced during the visit to Auschwitz was a huge shock. And I think that Auschwitz is a good example that war is a terrible thing that kills lots of innocent people.

Respect your neighbor no matter what ethnicity.... He is a person just like me and also feels pain, sadness, suffering, joy. Auschwitz taught us exactly that.

To the question of what we can learn from visiting Auschwitz, young people answered:

I think that Auschwitz shows us how cruel people can be. They murdered and condemned to great suffering, not only Jews and Poles, but also people of other nationalities, and even their own fellow countrymen. They thought that Germans were the best nation in the world and that people of other backgrounds don't have the right to live and therefore need to be exterminated.

The lesson in Auschwitz taught me to have respect for other people regardless of religion or nationality.

The lesson in Auschwitz taught me respect for people of other nations and to observe moral principles.

As illustrated by the answers of both the pupils and teachers, Auschwitz is most often perceived in universal terms as a symbol of genocide, although both groups are aware that the main and largest number of victims of the camp were Jews. The research acknowledged the necessity to verify whether young people really understand what the Holocaust meant and means for the Jewish nation, and what was the image of Jews among eighth-grade students. The research showed that young people perceived Jews as normal people, similar to themselves, although few had actually ever seen a Jew, at most "on television or in a museum." To a question about characteristic features of Jews, pupils listed: "different beliefs, caps on their heads, sideburns, and circumcision." One group expressed the conviction that Jews live "in Israel, Germany, England, the USA," and "really everywhere."

The majority had heard about Jews from their grandparents. The contents of these accounts included many negative stereotypes. Many had heard that Jews are "different from us," which stood in contrast with their own views, expressed earlier, "that they are people just like us." According to some, the difference was supposed to lie in the fact that Jews "are worse." Many students in the discussion did not agree with this view. Among answers to the question of whether the negative opinions they had heard about Jews were true, one said, "They could say the same about us."

At the end, to the question of whether they would like to meet young Jews, the group answered in unison, "Yes," arguing that they would like in this way "to get to know them, their traditions, and to learn something about them."

I think that facilitating this mutual acquaintance is the great task awaiting us all.

KRYSTYNA OLEKSY is deputy director of the Auschwitz-Birkenau State Museum in Oswiecim, responsible for education. She cooperates with the Yad Vashem Institute in Jerusalem, as well as with Polish and foreign high schools. She is the author of articles on the poetry and memoirs of prisoners at Auschwitz and co-author of the exhibition *Zanim odeszli* (Before They Perished).

STEFAN WILKANOWICZ

▶ 21. What do Poles who live near the places where thousands of people were killed feel?

Auschwitz awakens in me a particular fear, especially when I observe young people. Some come away practically broken, and I fear that they will leave there with only hatred and feelings of powerlessness. And others seem indifferent; after thousands of hours of watching violence and atrocities on television, can one still be concerned about anything, or does killing just become normal?

Polish family entering the Extermination Museum on the grounds of the former concentration camp in Auschwitz-Birkenau. Photo by T. Jodlowski/Forum

I can't speak for people who live near places where mass crimes were once committed. I can only speak for myself, acknowledging that I am not typical, because I have been involved for many years with issues relating to Auschwitz, but I do not live there. On the one hand, my involvement creates a closeness and, undoubtedly, a fuller understanding of the crime (its causes and its results), but on the other, it is to some extent desensitizing, because with frequent visits, one does not experience things as one did the first time. Further, my experiences can in no way be compared to those of former prisoners—theirs was a different world.

My unique perspective comes as well from spending communal nights of prayer with German penitents from *Aktion Suehnizeichen* (Action Reconciliation), who came to atone at the former camp for the crimes of their fellow countrymen, and then from working with them to clear the rubble of one of the crematoria. Among the group was a very young German girl whose father slapped her when he found out why she was going to Auschwitz.

Previous page: Majdanek concentration camp, seen against the background of buildings in Lublin. Courtesy of the Majdanek State Museum

Auschwitz awakens in me a particular fear, especially when I observe young people. Some come away practically broken, and I fear that they will leave there with only hatred and feelings of powerlessness. And others seem indifferent; after thousands of hours of watching violence and atrocities on television, can one still be concerned about anything, or does killing just become normal?

I am afraid, too, of ignorance—often prideful ignorance. Not long ago one of our friends asked a group of young Americans how they imagined the camp. A dead silence fell on the group, and finally someone said, "Well, they probably had only black-and-white televisions there." Of course, this is an extreme case, but the problem remains. It relates to much more than just adequate knowledge of fact, to understanding (to whatever extent possible) the phenomenon, and the ability to reach proper conclusions regarding new threats of hate and contempt as well as professional propaganda based on fear and disgust.

From here, Auschwitz is a continuous provocation to reflect on this memorial place that would caution, inspire action, offer orientation, unite people. Is that too much to ask? Perhaps it is, but it is necessary.

That is why events that influence people are so important. One such event that I participated in last year was among the most moving experiences of my life. Imagine a slow, silent procession of 500 Arabs and Jews along the ramp at Birkenau. We hear the names of victims, read aloud alternately by Jews and Arabs. I am walking between Archimandrate Emile Shoufani, the Melchite rector of Nazareth, and a Muslim cleric in exotic costume.

Where did they come from? Their presence was the fruit of many years of work by Father Shoufani, director of a school in Nazareth attended by Christian and Muslim children, a school with its own Jewish sister-school in Jerusalem. This is work in defiance of hatred growing everyday.

I dream of such an Auschwitz—a place of hope.

STEFAN WILKANOWICZ is an engineer, teacher, journalist, and editor-in-chief of *Znak* (Sign) magazine. For many years he was the president of the Catholic Intelligentsia Club in Cracow. Presently he is the president of the Christian Culture Foundation ZNAK, and vice-president of the International Council of the Auschwitz-Birkenau State Museum.

LAURENCE WEINBAUM

▶ 22. Why do Jews accuse Poles of complicity in the Shoah?

Survivors of the Holocaust in Poland often recount the indifference and hostility of the Polish populace. Jews who did survive thanks to the heroic efforts of Polish rescuers, whether in hiding or with false papers, also had to contend with the phenomenon of Poles who sought to unmask them, whether for pecuniary reasons or out of ingrained hatred.

In Jewish consciousness Poland is a land of bittersweet memories. Few countries of the Jewish Diaspora evoke the same depth of emotion. Since 1945 Poland has been seen by Jews, above all, as the epicenter of the Shoah, the charnel house of European Jewry, and the venue of unimaginable evil and suffering. Jews, taught from childhood the imperative to remember (*Zachor!*), are little different from others (including Poles) in their tendency to view historical events in a simplistic way, devoid of nuance. Moreover, the Jewish public remains to a large extent ignorant of the history of the many centuries of Jewish life in Poland, with its glorious and inglorious eras, that preceded the rise of Adolf Hitler.

Undoubtedly, many Jews share the sentiments expressed by Henryk Grynberg, who wrote of Poland:

Here more of them died than had been born
Here they have left more than they ever had
Here there is more bread from their ashes
Than they had ever eaten.

That is so even if they have never heard of this Polish-born Jewish writer and his work.

Indeed, in Jewish circles, Poles are often seen (much to their dismay, and often to their amazement) as accessories to the crime, if not prime perpetrators. At best, they are viewed as indifferent bystanders who were not unhappy that the Germans (despite the misery they were inflicting on the Poles) were at least bringing about a long-desired *Judenfrei* Poland. And there is a vast body of survivor testimony to corroborate that view.

Thus, Yitzhak Shamir, one of Israel's Polish-born former prime ministers, whose father was murdered by Polish neighbors, could claim that Poles "ingest anti-Semitism with their mother's milk." This is a view that is reflected in literature and film and has found wide credence beyond the Jewish street.

In the period leading to the outbreak of World War II, which some observers view as a prelude to the horrors to come, anti-Semitism be-

Previous page: Prayers for the people murdered in Jedwabne, July 2001.
Photo by C. Fissel

Two cities: Jews crossing the bridge over Chlodna Street from the small to the large ghetto, while normal life goes on around them in Warsaw, 1942.
Courtesy of the Jewish Historical Institute

came a dominant force in Polish society. Jews were seen as an undesirable and superfluous element. In September 1938, just a year before the German invasion of Poland, the Polish ambassador to Germany, Jozef Lipski, reported to the Foreign Ministry that Hitler had discussed with him the possibility of solving the Jewish problem in Central Europe by their emigration to overseas colonies. "I told him," wrote Lipski, "that if he finds such a solution, we will erect him a beautiful monument in Warsaw." Furthermore, the Roman Catholic Church, which has traditionally played a strong role in Polish society, contributed to poisoning Polish minds with the virus of anti-Semitism. Given the atrocities that came with the German occupation, that prewar obsession with Jews cast Poles in a particularly negative light and reinforced the notion that they were partly responsible for the terrible fate of Polish Jewry.

Not surprisingly, the widely held Jewish perception of Poles has nothing in common with the way Poles see themselves—as heroes of a ferocious struggle in which they battled the German occupiers and as "the country that did not produce a Quisling." The average Polish "man on the street" has yet to confront the fact that in wartime Poland one could both participate in the destruction of Jews *and* fight against the Germans. For many Poles there was no contradiction in this. Even the citizens of the infamous town of Jedwabne, which the late Father Stanislaw Musial described as a "new name for the Holocaust," akin to Auschwitz, did not and do not see themselves as having done the Germans' bidding. This bitter truth was reflected in the powerful novella *Wielki Tydzien* (Holy Week), written in 1943 by the Polish author Jerzy Andrzejewski and published just after the war. While the ghetto is in flames, one of the protagonists, Zalewski, declares:

> I tell you that in this case we can be grateful to Hitler. He has done a very difficult job for us—let us say frankly, a very unpleasant, dirty job. Now there won't be any more Jewish problem! If Hitler hadn't done it for us, after the war we should have had to liquidate the surviving Jews.

Survivors of the Holocaust in Poland often recount the indifference and hostility of the Polish populace. Jews who did survive thanks to the heroic efforts of Polish rescuers, whether in hiding or with forged "Aryan" papers, also had to contend with the phenomenon of Poles who sought to unmask them, whether for pecuniary reasons or out of ingrained hatred. There can be little doubt that more Jews would have survived had Poles turned a blind eye to the Jews hiding in their midst.

On the other hand, Jews today do not always take into consideration the existential dangers implicit in hiding Jews in occupied Poland and generally attribute the failure to rescue larger numbers as clear evidence that Poles were anti-Semitic. That the Germans elected to build the death camps on Polish soil is often cited in Jewish circles, quite groundlessly, as "proof" of Polish anti-Semitism. The fact that the camps are often carelessly referred to as "Polish death camps" has obviously not helped matters.

That local Poles sometimes dispatched returning survivors of the cataclysm only served to reinforce the image of Poles as hopeless and, at times, murderous anti-Semites. That pogroms could take place after the Holocaust is seen as the best evidence that "Poles are the worst anti-Semites" and "even worse than the Germans." Successive waves of postwar anti-Semitism, which led to an exodus of most of the highly assimilated Jewish remnant, strengthened this image of Poles as implacable anti-Semites. Moreover, Polish society's failure to come to grips with the wartime history of Polish-Jewish relations, the attempt to excise the Jews from the general history of Poland, and especially attempts to "appropriate the Holocaust" by posthumously granting Jews who perished as Jews the status of Poles have also left a very bitter taste. As Paul Lendvai pungently observed in his book *Anti-Semitism Without Jews*, "Dead Jews make good Poles."

It must be recognized that the preponderance of Jews of Polish origin throughout the world, both in relative numbers and in Jewish public life, has ensured that the story of the Shoah in Poland is better known than that of other communities. That Germans worked assiduously to convince the world that the Holocaust was perpetrated by "Nazis" rather than by "Germans" has also had its impact. It is not uncommon to read about "Nazis, Poles, and Jews" with all too predictable results.

In recent years, especially since the collapse of Communism, there has been an enormous change. In the wake of the revelations about Jedwabne and even earlier, Polish society has begun to address the ambiguities of its history. Jews, too, have begun to recognize the mistake of looking at the thousand-year history of Polish-Jewish coexistence through the narrow prism of the Holocaust.

On the other hand, the curriculum of many of the study trips by Jewish youngsters to Poland in the last fifteen years has strengthened some of the prevailing stereotypes, reinforcing the idea that Poland = Auschwitz. There have been a sufficient number of anti-Semitic incidents (graffiti, cat calls, and vandalism) to leave a negative impression—and one suspects that some of the participants are not disappointed by that fact. In recent years, however, the organizers of these pilgrimages have adopted a more sensitive, balanced approach, moving away from the idea that the Polish-Jewish experience began and ended with the gas chambers of Treblinka.

Certainly, with the passage of time, a more dispassionate approach to Polish-Jewish relations could emerge. To be sure, relations between Poles and Jews will always be overshadowed by history, the only question is how that history will be interpreted.

DR. LAURENCE WEINBAUM is a senior research officer at the Research Institute of the World Jewish Congress in Jerusalem and a lecturer in history at the College of Judea and Samaria in Ariel.

WLADYSLAW BARTOSZEWSKI

▶ 23. Are there people in Poland who deny the Holocaust?

Outright negation of the Nazi crimes, including the Nazi crimes against the Jews, is a punishable offense in Polish law. While the so-called "Auschwitz lie" has thus far resulted in one court case, the phenomenon on a societal scale is nevertheless not particularly threatening, because since 1989, the media of the new democratic Polish Republic have played a generally positive role in dealing with issues of historical truth.

Knowledge about the facts of the German crimes committed during the occupation of Poland was, in general, substantially greater than knowledge of these crimes in other European countries occupied by the Germans, for three decades after the war. The widespread knowledge was due, above all, to the extent of the terror against both Jews and the Polish Christian population, and the surviving victims' testimonies about their experiences. A few statistics on Poland's losses during the years of World War II are instructive: Among those killed were approximately one fourth of the priests and professors at institutions of higher learning, more than half of the lawyers, and approximately 15 percent of the teachers.

This situation created enhanced awareness of the extent of the Nazi crimes. Thus, it was specifically in Poland that public trials, resulting in judgments and the imposition of the death penalty, were carried against the following groups and individuals: the garrison of Majdanek (1944); some of the personnel of Auschwitz-Birkenau, as well as the camp commandant, Rudolph Hoess (1947); the staff of the camp of Stutthof (1946); Gauleiter (regional branch leader) Arthur Greiser (1946), who ran the Lodz Ghetto; Ludwig Fischer, the district governor of Warsaw (1947), who controlled the Warsaw Ghetto; the chief of the so-called government in Cracow, Joseph Buhler (1948); the executioners of the Lodz ghetto (Hans Biebow, 1947) and the camp at Cracow-Plaszow (Amon Goeth, 1948). These and other Nazi trials, in which Jewish prisoners testified as witnesses, were widely reported through newspapers and radio broadcasts. Already in 1947 the decision was made to establish a permanent protection of the grounds of Auschwitz-Birkenau as a site of memory, and a national museum was also created there. Today, this is an important center of education and publishing, which has been working in close collaboration with Yad Vashem in Jerusalem and the U.S. Holocaust Memorial Museum in Washington, D.C., for more than ten years.

Generational changes have created challenges in educating today's youth about recent history, including that of World War II—in Poland as in other European countries. The "revisionist" theories of Robert Faurisson and David Irving, leading to Holocaust denial, have flowed into Poland (if belatedly) from Western Europe, but are still

---

Previous page: Crematorium at the grounds of the Majdanek camp. Courtesy of the Majdanek State Museum

generally completely unknown to the majority of Poles. Outright negation of the Nazi crimes, including the Nazi crimes against the Jews, is a punishable offense in Polish law. While the so-called "Auschwitz lie" has thus far resulted in one court case, the phenomenon on a societal scale is nevertheless not particularly threatening, because since 1989, the media of the new democratic Polish Republic have played a generally positive role in dealing with issues of historical truth. Furthermore, in libraries and bookstores hundreds of titles dealing with the history of the Holocaust are available, and the market has shown great interest in some memoirs. Given how much information is accessible, fleeting cases of denial of the historical truth are barely noticeable.

PROF. WLADYSLAW BARTOSZEWSKI is a historian, former Polish minister of foreign affairs, co-founder of the Polish *Zegota* Council for Aid to Jews, holder of the "Righteous Among the Nations distinction," participant in the Warsaw Uprising of 1944, and former prisoner of KL Auschwitz. He is also the director of the International Auschwitz Council for the Polish Government, and an honorary citizen of the State of Israel.

Gate at the entrance to KL Auschwitz I carrying the infamous inscription, "Arbeit macht frei." Photo by R. Szuchta

Elzbieta Isakiewicz

▶ 24. Do Poles feel disturbed by the monuments built in memory of the Holocaust?

In Poland, which the Germans chose as the main site of the Holocaust—and which they turned into a hell during the war—monuments, obelisks, and tablets memorializing the murder and suffering of victims are to be found at every turn. No one here is surprised; such objects bear witness to history.

Monument to the victims of the Lodz Ghetto at the Radegast railway station.
Courtesy of the City of Lodz Office

As far as I know, there is no sociological research on precisely this question. Nevertheless, in 2000, one study asked what is the attitude of Poles toward the desecration of Jewish cemeteries. Among the respondents, 93 percent unconditionally condemned the act, and 80 percent demanded legal pursuit of the culprits. And one might, it seems, view monuments commemorating the Holocaust as, in some sense, cemeteries. A sociologist might be satisfied with this answer. But as a reporter, a professional observer of reality, I will allow myself some additional reflections.

In Poland, which the Germans chose as the main site of the Holocaust—and which they turned into a hell during the war—monuments, obelisks, and tablets memorializing the murder and suffering of victims are to be found at every turn. No one here is surprised; such objects bear witness to history. They have become part of the landscape; each successive generation grows up simply accustomed to their presence. Here there is no way to deny that the Holocaust happened, that a war took place in which Jews and Poles died. That, in my opin-

<hr />

Previous page: Monument to the victims of the Warsaw Ghetto, modern Warsaw. Photo by B. Osser

ion, is the attitude of most Poles. It is the norm, one could say. If a problem exists, it is marginal.

There is something else, however, that may indeed be a specifically Polish phenomenon: People who feel inundated by accusations against Poles for complicity in the Holocaust may look askance at Holocaust monuments, because every new monument honoring the suffering of Jews would appear to them to be belittling Polish suffering and Polish contributions to the fight against the occupiers. It was particularly visible under Communism. The memorial of the Warsaw Ghetto Uprising was erected in Warsaw shortly after the war, as early as in the 1940s. To have a memorial to the Warsaw Uprising of 1944—which reaped incomparably more victims—the Poles had to wait until the 1990s, when the Communist regime collapsed.

Nevertheless, we may trust that neither the first type, the incorrigible anti-Semite, nor the second, the competitor for national suffering— while they must be resisted—threaten the memory intended to be preserved by the monuments. This is so primarily because in recent years the challenge of Polish-Jewish dialogue has taken root on both sides, among people of good will, open to the truth and to their fellow human beings.

ELZBIETA ISAKIEWICZ is a journalist who writes on Jewish history in Poland and Polish-Jewish relations. She is the author of *Czerwony ołówek. O Polaku, który uratował tysiące Żydów* (Red Pencil: About a Pole Who Saved Thousands of Jews) and *Ustna harmonijka. Relacje Żydów, których od Zagłady uratowali Polacy* (Harmonica: Jews Relate How Poles Saved Them from the Holocaust).

MIRIAM AKAVIA

▶ 25. What do Jews who left Poland think about their country of origin?

Jews and Poles can discover much in common. This shared history can be found at every step in Poland. What we find is often painful, but—at least for the majority of us—also near and very dear.

It is not easy to answer this question because there are many kinds of Jews: those from the city and from small towns, educated and *amej aracot* (simple people), religious and secular, Bundists and Zionists, socialists and capitalists. And, of course, if these different orientations weren't enough, each person has his or her own individual relationship to Poland and thinks differently about it. Other important factors might be one's age, or rather date of birth, and more importantly, the date when one left Poland.

It would be simplest for me to answer by telling how I, Miriam Akavia, think about Poland. But I know that not everyone was born, as I was, in beautiful Cracow; not all were brought up in a family that, while maintaining Jewish tradition, revered Polish literature, poetry, and painting. Not all parents instilled in their children an affection for their surroundings: the scents of the Polish spring, the Polish rivers that murmured, and forests that gave generous shade in summer. In autumn the trees became golden, and in winter, in our cozy childhood bedrooms, we looked through the window at the enchanting flakes of snow.

Love for this world is not erased, even by the terrible reality of the Holocaust, with its collapse of all human norms, indescribable bestiality and evil. And who knows? Perhaps the very norms ingrained in us during youth helped us to survive the worst of times and provided strength for a lifetime.

We know that for hundreds of years Poland was where the largest group of Jews could be found. Persecuted in the West and in the East, in Poland they found a place to settle and to stay. For centuries ruled by other nations that tore it apart, Poland during the interwar period—its scarcely twenty years of independence—was a multicultural country where, despite difficult moments, Jewish life blossomed: *heders, yeshivot,* Hebrew schools, Tarbut schools, Tachkemoni, Jewish youth organizations ranging from right to left in their political orientations, Jewish creativity in three languages (Polish, Hebrew, and Yiddish), and Zionist *hachshara* programs (preparation centers for *aliya,* or settling in Israel).

←

Previous page: Miriam Akavia with friends in Israel.
Miriam Akavia collection

Childhood in Cracow: Miriam
Akavia (on a chair), with siblings.
Miriam Akavia collection

Thus, to me it was strange to hear from Polish Jews who came
to Israel as *halutzim* (pioneers) that they felt no nostalgia or desire
to return to the country from which they came. Perhaps this represents an indoctrinated feeling of restraint, a behavior evoked from
the past. The Zionist ideologues of that time (David Ben-Gurion, Zeev
Jabotinsky) wanted to invent a new kind of Jew, which meant disas-
sociating themselves from the humiliation of the Diaspora, skipping
over two thousand years of history to connect to their biblical ancestors. Such was the educational orientation in Palestine at that time;
perhaps, also, some *halutzim* had had bad experiences at Polish universities—which was not my experience.

Those saved from the Shoah had different experiences. It was
a source of great pain that when they arrived in Israel, no one understood them. They were suspected of being weak, of lacking dignity,
and worse yet. The survivors can be divided into three groups: First,
there were those who survived the terrible times thanks to the help
of Poles; they surely must feel gratitude and love toward their rescuers,
and thus, to a large extent, to Poland as well. It needs to be stressed
that in Poland a person who helped a Jew during the German occupation could be condemned to death, together with his entire family, and
yet despite this dreadful sentence—which in many cases was carried
out—the largest number of the Righteous Among the Nations were
from Poland. A second group includes those who suffered during the
war at the hands of Poles: They were turned in, robbed, blackmailed,
and in some cases, members of their families were even killed by Poles.
These people often generalize and feel hatred toward Poles and Poland

as a whole. A third group is people who felt and feel pain and regret at the indifference of the surrounding population to their fate. This indifference on the part of their neighbors, schoolmates, and army buddies at times hurt more than the most hideous barbarity and terrible crimes carried out by the "alien" Germans.

Polish Jews living in Israel today who attempted to stay in Poland and rebuild their ruined lives there after the Second World War had yet different experiences. These people were generally (but not exclusively) repatriated from the Soviet Union. Miraculously saved, they were faced with new demoralization and dehumanization upon their return to Poland, which was itself battered and oppressed, in which a shared Polish-Jewish history became an irony that toyed brutally with our fates. The Russians, the liberators of the Jews, were now the new occupiers of Poland—a state of affairs that caused great tension and misunderstanding. Nevertheless, postwar Poland was, for many of these repatriates, a surrogate fatherland; it educated whole cadres of Jews, enabled them to enjoy freedom of profession, and instilled in them a new love of Poland. This love ultimately revealed itself as the manipulative politics of the Communist government, and after Gomulka's time, many Jews decided to sever their ties and start new lives in Israel. Finally, love for Poland was brutally disappointed in 1968.

But disillusioned love does not always die. For the past few decades, Poland has been a free country. The bulk of the historical research and scholarly work, publications, and books on Jewish themes written in Polish emanate from present-day Poland. Today, when one can write and speak openly, when compromising events are no longer avoided, and history is not being falsifed, Jews and Poles can discover much in common. This shared history can be found at every step in Poland. What we find is often painful, but—at least for the majority of us—also near and very dear.

MIRIAM AKAVIA is an Israeli writer born in Cracow, and a Holocaust survivor saved by "Aryan papers." During World War II she was confined to the Cracow ghetto, imprisoned at Plaszow, later transferred to KL Auschwitz-Birkenau, and KL Bergen-Belsen. She is the author of youth literature and memoirs, and her books have been translated into 13 languages. She is a founder and president of the Polish-Israeli Friendship Society, and a member of the Commission at Yad Vashem responsible for bestowing the title of Righteous Among the Nations.

Present-Day Poland
and the Jews

Andrzej Folwarczny

▶ 26. How are current relations between Poles and Jews from abroad?

In Jewish communities the common conviction is that Poles looked upon the Holocaust with indifference, and sometimes even actively took part in the extermination of the Jews. From the other side, Polish memory is focused mainly on Polish suffering and the heroism of Righteous Poles who saved Jews during World War II.

The political changes that took place in Poland in 1989 bore many fruits, among them the renewal of diplomatic relations between Poland and Israel. During the past few decades Poland has become one of Israel's most important political partners in Europe.

Despite this, relations between ordinary people—Poles and Jews —confront us with deeply rooted stereotypes. History has an enormous influence on present-day Polish-Jewish relations. Poland is the place where the Holocaust happened, and it is mainly for this reason that Polish-Jewish relations are, and will remain, unique. Before the war 3.5 million Jews lived in Poland. More than 90 percent of them were exterminated by the Germans during World War II. The tragic memories of those who survived were aggravated by postwar events, like the Kielce pogrom in 1946 or the anti-Semitic events of March 1968.

Poles and Jews formed completely different pictures of Polish-Jewish relations during World War II and after its end. Sometimes one has the impression that among Poles and Jews there are simply two widespread, yet totally contradictory versions of the history of Polish-Jewish relations during the war. In Jewish communities the common conviction is that Poles looked upon the Holocaust with indifference, and sometimes even actively took part in the extermination of the Jews. From the other side, Polish memory is focused mainly on Polish suffering and the heroism of Righteous Poles who saved Jews during the war.

It's hard to feel surprised at these different narratives. In postwar Poland the study of history was subjected to Communist propaganda, resulting in an entire generation of Poles deprived of reliable education about the recent history of their country, including World War II and the Holocaust. Only in recent years has it begun to sink into Polish public opinion how very complicated Polish-Jewish wartime relations were. Among Jews, on the other hand, knowledge about Poland is based mainly on the accounts of parents and grandparents who were forced to leave Poland. Poland often appears in such recollections only as the site of the extermination of the Jewish nation and as a country inhabited by people hostile toward Jews. This negative picture generally undergoes change only through confrontation with the reality of present-day Poland.

<hr>

Previous page: Meeting of young Poles and Jews in a high school in Warsaw organized by the Forum for Dialogue Among Nations. Photo by Klaudia Kiercz

Next page: March of the Living in Oswiecim. Photo by P. Turecki

Many mutual prejudices derive from a lack of knowledge. Often negative stereotypes are sustained by educational materials and school textbooks. In order to overcome this, at the beginning of the 1990s the governments of Poland and Israel created a joint commission made up of Polish and Israeli historians. The work of the commission was to verify the contents of Polish and Israeli textbooks concerning their mutual relations. Despite the fact that the commission completed its work in 1995, until today, newly prepared textbooks (both Polish and Israeli) have in most cases not taken its recommendations into consideration.

Aside from education, contacts between Poles and Jews from abroad are exceptionally important in overcoming the existing biases. Only direct contact offers an occasion to confront stereotypes with reality. This is particularly true for the younger generation. At present, contacts between young Poles and Jews are only sporadic. The geographic distance separating Poland from large groups of Jewish people inhibits such meetings. The high costs involved in organizing youth exchange programs mean that they are a rarity.

Nevertheless, every year over twenty thousand young Israelis and Jews from other countries come to Poland in the context of programs whose goal is to acquaint them with the tragedy of the Holocaust. The overwhelming majority of them visit extermination camps, but have virtually no contact with present-day Poland or with their Polish contemporaries. In such programs Poland is presented more as a national cemetery than as the country of their ancestors. Further, young Jews often have the opportunity to see anti-Semitic graffiti on walls that Poles walk by in total indifference. Thus, they return from Poland with the same stereotypes with which they came, often even more deeply ingrained.

Very few groups meet with Polish youth. These groups represent the hope for the future. Perhaps the younger generation of Poles and Jews will overcome the existing prejudices and, while remembering the difficulties of the past, will concentrate on building a better future. In order for this to happen, though, we must offer them adequate conditions.

ANDRZEJ FOLWARCZNY is the president and the founder of the Forum for Dialogue Among Nations. He was formerly a member of the Polish Parliament (Sejm) and then the chairman of the Polish-Israeli Parliamentary Group.

IRENEUSZ KRZEMINSKI

▶ 27. Are Poles anti-Semites?

Anti-Semites believe that Jews *always*
attempt to rule over others (although never
pursuing this goal openly, but rather *always* in
secret), that Jews have special talents
and/or are known for their ability to acquire wealth
and financial control over the world, and that they
display a powerful solidarity such that one Jew
always feels connected to others, even if they come
from different parts of the world.

This question sounds quite provocative, especially to the ears of a sociologist. Yet this was what we titled our 1992 book, which reported on the results of the first systematic opinion poll on the topic of Polish anti-Semitism. The title referred to discussions that emerged in the first half of the 1990s about the stereotype of Poles as traditional anti-Semites and nationalists. Particularly memorable in this context, and picked up by the global media, was a statement made by an important Israeli politician (former Israeli prime minister Yitzhak Shamir) that Poles absorb anti-Semitism with their mothers' milk. For a significant segment of Polish society, this expression was rather shocking, and I must admit that for myself and my colleagues—researchers, including many from Jewish families—it was not pleasant news. Yet the headlines revealed nothing more than a confrontation of stereotypes.

As members of the March '68 generation who, as youths, had ourselves faced state-sponsored anti-Semitism under Wladyslaw Gomulka's Polish People's Republic, we decided to undertake research that would speak reliably to the question of anti-Semitism in Poland. The research turned out to be very important. The sociological survey carried out in 1989-90 by the American Jewish Committee in Poland, Hungary, and then Czechoslovakia indicated that anti-Semitic statements were made in Poland most frequently of the three countries examined at the onset of democratic transformation.

We agreed from the start that we should categorize as *traditional anti-Semitism* an attitude of antipathy toward Jews justified by religious beliefs (e.g., the Jews killed Christ), and that such attitudes would likely be relatively infrequent. They have survived, though, despite the official change of stance by the postwar Catholic Church toward Jews and the Jewish religion (particularly the Second Vatican Council, which acknowledged that Jews should not be held guilty for a sentence ordered by a Roman). Seeing Jews as Christ-killers was the accepted view among Christians, including Catholics, for centuries. It is therefore unsurprising that such views are held, for the most part, by older people with little education living largely in the country and in small villages—often in the eastern regions of Poland. These data have remained constant, ap-

←——————————————————————————————————————

Previous page: Wooden sculptures of the so-called "Jew with a coin"—a popular item in contemporary Polish souvenir shops believed to bring luck in the financial activity. Some regard them as harmless, but others consider them a representation of an anti-Semitic stereotype. Photo by Erica Lehrer

Poster on a street in Cracow with the inscription: "New lords of Poland!!! Privatize Poland's assets—only for them!" Photo by L. Weinbaum

pearing unchanged ten years later, in 2002, in research that replicated the original 1992 study.

We then delineated another category, *modern anti-Semitism* (according to Helena Datner's typology). We described it as antipathy toward Jews justified by anti-Semitic political ideology. Based on beliefs about the power and influence of Jews on the activities of the nation-state and on the world at large, modern anti-Semitism began to spread across Europe after the French Revolution. According to our survey, this conviction—often appearing as part of nationalist programs—is the dominant strain of anti-Semitic attitudes in Poland. Anti-Semites of this type believe that Jews *always* attempt to rule over others (although never pursuing this goal openly, but rather *always* in secret), that Jews have special talents and/or are known for their ability to acquire wealth and financial control over the world, and that they display a powerful solidarity, such that one Jew *always* feels connected to others, even if they come from different parts of the world. Frequently included in this ideological canon of "knowledge about Jews" are accusations that Jews are sympathetic to Communism. This stands, to be sure, in contradiction to accusations that Jews are in control of capital, but such details have not—and will not—disturb anti-Semitic ideologues in the least. In Poland, this ideology was associated with the National Democracy movement of the Second Republic—in short, "Endecja."

This type of anti-Semitism was the most prevalent among the subjects of our research. In the space of a decade it appears that attitudes of hatred and hostility toward Jews also increased markedly, from approximately 17 percent in 1992 to over 27 percent in 2002. These results leave no doubt that the image of the Jew in the Polish mind has worsened overall. To the same extent that positive characteristics dominated the Polish national stereotype of Jews in 1992, negative ones came to dominate in 2002. In fact, our survey revealed an increase in hostile attitudes toward many other nations besides Jews, including Americans, toward whom there had been no such criticism in 1992. Thus, in 2002, one could speak with reasonable certainty of an increase in nationalistic hatreds and the emergence of xenophobia, or hatred towards all "others."

Our method of researching anti-Semitic attitudes allowed us to develop an indicator we called "anti-anti-Semitism." It suggested itself through negative answers to questions that contained anti-Semitic accusations, which the subject rejected. A significant strengthening of anti-Semitic attitudes in the latter survey was paralleled by a two-fold increase in anti-anti-Semitic attitudes since 1992, suggesting, above all, a pronounced polarization of attitudes among Poles. Answers on the 2002 survey showed a significant drop in the percentage of many types of ambivalence or ignorance, and additional research clearly distinguished among those who held attitudes of animosity toward Jews and those who, by contrast, thought it unwise or unacceptable to revive well-worn anti-Jewish stereotypes.

In 2002—as in 1992—the level of education had a clear-cut influence on traditional anti-Semitic attitudes, but that relationship did not hold for modern anti-Semitism. Higher levels of education, nevertheless, did have an impact on attitudes: the higher the level of education a person had attained, the more frequently would they declare "anti-anti-Semitic" attitudes. However, in 2002, our 1992 thesis that the impact of an educated individual's religiosity differed greatly from that of an uneducated individual was revealed as incorrect, at least in relation to their attitudes toward other nations. Declarations of deep faith as well as regular observance of religious practice significantly correlated with a percent of the self-described anti-Semites of the modern type.

"Atheistic" anti-Semitism also appeared: A significant segment of the post-Communist left (the SLD, the Democratic Left Alliance) is comprised of people of decidedly anti-Semitic inclination. In 1992, similarly, the post-Communist electorate (at that time, SdRP, Social Democracy of the Republic of Poland, voters) was clearly split into anti-Semites and anti-anti-Semites. Nevertheless, the connection of anti-Semitic attitudes with religion and the Church did not weaken. In fact, quite the opposite occurred, as the category of "traditional anti-Semite" overlaps almost completely with those who constitute the core believing listeners of Radio Maria. The very presence of this radio station in the public arena, along with a variety of anti-Semitic and xenophobic trends evidenced during the campaigns accompanying Poland's accession to the European Union, and the presence of political manifestations firmly in the Endecja tradition are among the factors contributing to the increase in anti-Semitic attitudes.

Still, this significant rise in open declarations of anti-Semitism, as well as an increase in markedly less favorable images of Jews in comparison with earlier measures, suggests that other factors are at work. For Poles, the symbol of "the Jew" has consequences for the definition of their own identity, similar to the symbol of "the German." One could put it colloquially this way: A Pole is not like a Jew or a German, who always tries to act in his own interest, but rather a Pole keeps his promises, even if it means going against his own interest. This competitive posture toward Jews results in the conviction among many of those surveyed that in the contemporary world, the current memory of the past—including the wartime and the postwar era—has been completely dominated by the Jewish tragedy of the Holocaust. The Jews have taken possession of the image of the past, and thus no one remembers the suffering of others. Most importantly, no one remembers the victimization of the Poles, who are instead seen as Nazi collaborators. This view is so painful to the Polish consciousness that it leads to a changed assessment of the past and an increase in hostility toward Jews, who this time are to blame for holding a "monopoly on suffering." Key to such discourses is the notion that it is precisely the perspective of the suffering of Poles—always a noble suffering, of course—that should dominate the image of history. Thus, anti-Semitic declarations are to a large degree treated as a legitimate defense and an indication of disagreement with the image of the past which—however exaggerated—is seen as the one held by world public opinion. Anti-Jewish attitudes are thus a key mechanism by which the desire for recognition of Polish wartime and post-war suffering is manifested. Jews—or rather some symbolic image of the Jewish nation—thus appear as in competition for the mantle of righteous suffering, incurred as a result of the moral national demeanor during an era of terrible experiences of historic proportions.

IRENEUSZ KRZEMINSKI is a sociologist, professor at the Institute of Sociology at Warsaw University, and deputy rector of the Jerzy Giedroyc High School of Communication and Social Media in Warsaw. He has done research on political transformations and anti-Semitism in Poland and Ukraine. He is the author of *Czy Polacy są antysemitami?* (Are Poles Anti-Semites?) and *Antysemityzm w Polsce i na Ukrainie: Raport z badań* (Anti-Semitism in Poland and Ukraine: Research Report) as well as works on interaction theory.

MARCIN KORNAK

▶ 28. Why are there so many anti-Semitic graffiti on the walls in Polish cities?

People in Poland, the majority of them, are simply not bothered by anti-Semitic graffiti. Even if it does disturb them, it does not do so to the extent that they would protest against it.
It is difficult to imagine that the slogan *"Jews to the gas"* actually upsets or offends someone if they see it multiple times a day and don't feel any imperative to do something about it.

I wonder about this often when I see some particularly offensive slo-gans that have remained for years on the facade of a building—some-times even on a government institution—in the center of a large city. It leads me to one conclusion: People in Poland, the majority of them, are simply not bothered by anti-Semitic graffiti. Even if it does disturb them, it does not do so to the extent that they would protest against it. It is difficult to imagine that the slogan "Jews to the gas" actually upsets or offends someone if they see it multiple times a day and don't feel any imperative to do something about it. Indifference to such words—and all that lies behind them—is a glaring blemish on the portrait of the Polish nation.

We could easily distinguish other spheres of values, themes, or ideas, which, if offended, would evoke in Poles much more frequent, decisive, and, thus, more effective reactions. Unfortunately, the propagation of anti-Semitism does not give rise to such reactions among the majority of Poles.

In Issue #14 of the journal *Never Again*, published by our association of the same name (*Nigdy Wiecej*), we printed images of anti-Semitic slo-gans and drawings found on the barrack walls at Auschwitz-Birkenau. I do not know which is more frightening—that someone was able to do this kind of vandalism in such a place (but maybe this should not be so very surprising, considering that people were capable of carrying out the *Endlosung* itself), or that some of these graffiti have been there for decades!

Such passivity in the face of anti-Semitic expression on the walls of Polish cities, towns, and in the countryside is clearly only a part of a broader phenomenon: the longstanding indifference and hostility of a large proportion of Poles toward Jews, which has left a deep imprint on Polish history, culture, and the present.

I believe that the basic cause of this indifference toward anti-Semitic graffiti, and, in part, also toward the fate of the Jews some sixty years ago, can be found in the history of the coexistence of Poles and Jews. Although, as a rule this coexistence proceeded peacefully, it was none-theless a case of two parallel streams, often independent of one another. It would be difficult to speak of shared experiences in history, because they comprised, de facto, the histories of two separate worlds: the world

---

Previous page: Anti-Semitic inscription on a wall: "Hitler come back! Gas the Jews." Photo by D. Pach/Forum

of the Polish Christian majority, which kept a thoroughgoing distance from their "elder brothers in faith" (a euphemistic, and relatively new term used to refer to the Jewish people), and the world of the Jewish Diaspora, in which assimilation began quite late—only in the second half of the nineteenth century—and even then, only among the intellectual fringes.

From the very beginning of the formation of the modern Polish nation, the Jewish community was left on the margins of this process, while the Polish people developed its core values from two power sources: the intelligentsia (originating from the nobility) and the Catholic Church. Only after the failed uprising of January 1863 did the peasant masses begin to participate in this process. However, the Jews were neither its subject nor its object, displaying no particular activity in the support of statehood or any kind of determination to participate in the building of the Polish nation. In this way, they never became part of "us." Further, they were marked with the stigma of "otherness," which, along with the increase in nationalistic tendencies among the Polish part of the populace, began to take on ever more negative tones.

It is sad yet symptomatic that the Polish sense of trauma after World War II did not concern, or at least not to any great extent, the tragedy of the Shoah. Even such an extreme and dramatic event could not break the barrier of foreignness encircling Polish Jews. It suffices to recall the

Vandalized New Jewish Cemetery in Lomza, June 1994. Inscription: "The place of death where Jews were murdered by Nazis, 1941-1945."
Photo by Y. Reisner/The Jewish Historical Institute

Anti-Semitic inscription.
Photo by P. Herzog

bloody anti-Semitic events that took place in Kielce, in Cracow, and in Podhale just after the war's end, or the forced exodus of March 1968—really a pogrom, as Adam Michnik and Henryk Grynberg have not unreasonably called it. It is difficult to maintain that such events caused shock or opposition among the majority of Poles, and though numerous acts of solidarity undoubtedly took place, they did not emerge as a serious force, and rarely spilled beyond the circles of the cultural elite.

Is it any wonder, then, that "trivial" crimes, such as anti-Semitic graffiti, do not mobilize appropriate reactions by the Polish state or society? It is difficult to summon up impulses of solidarity and empathy for people who are different, and the "otherness" of Polish Jews was, and unfortunately continues to be, seen in a negative light.

This distance and negativity are present on the deepest levels of Polish culture. The Polish language is steeped in it. The emotional charge against Jews that reveals itself in the Polish colloquial, and even literary, language is clear. And it is in language that one's entire attitude toward the world and reality is encoded.

I am reminded of symptomatic events that occurred in 1998 in Lodz. The police caught two fourteen-year-old culprits who had desecrated a synagogue by painting it with swastikas. According to many, the fact that the incident was carried out by such frivolous delinquents was evidence of its insignificance. It was seen as run-of-the-mill vandalism by

Vandalized New Jewish Cemetery in Lomza, June 1994. Inscription "Jews out of Poland!" Photo by. Y. Reisner/The Jewish Historical Institute

thoughtless teenagers. But any logical, thoughtful, sensitive person sees that this very fact is evidence of the seriousness of the situation. If even children are consumed by anti-Semitic lunacy, it should be cause for alarm, not complacency.

The question remains: Is it possible to change this state of affairs? Surely it is. Doing so is the task of educators, community authorities, churches, culture brokers, social and political actors, and the government, but also of each so-called "normal person," because it is precisely in the field of everyday life that the effects of anti-Semitic prejudices lie. Changing this state of things will not occur quickly, but it will happen—if only people who value truth, good will, and respect for others continue to struggle with these problems. The difficulty of this task is no excuse not to dedicate oneself to it. Indeed, precisely the opposite.

MARCIN KORNAK is a poet and rock writer. He is the founder of Grupa Anty-Nazistowska (Anti-Nazi Group) and cofounder and president of the NIGDY WIECEJ (Never Again) Association, dealing with the problems of racism, neo-fascism and xenophobia. He is editor-in-chief of the magazine *Nigdy Wiecej* (Never Again), and also created the anti-fascist sports magazine *Stadion* (Stadium). He initiated the campaigns: "Music against Racism Not Dead," "Let's Kick Racism Out of the Stadiums." Since the age of fifteen, he has been living in a wheelchair.

ZUZANNA RADZIK

▶ 29. Do young people in Poland fight against anti-Semitism?

The majority is always passive—not out of ill will, but because they simply don't think anti-Semitism is a problem. Does "fighting" have to imply a specific activity? In my opinion, a fight is any public opposition or dissent from any free expression of anti-Semitic viewpoints.

It's hard to talk about a couple of million young people. Do they fight against anti-Semitism? The majority surely does not; the majority is always passive—not out of ill will, but because they simply don't think anti-Semitism is a problem. Perhaps they haven't encountered it in their own local environment, or they see it as just an odd but unthreatening viewpoint. There are, of course, unfortunately, those who identify in some way with anti-Semitic views. But those who underestimate the problem or simply are not aware of it make up the distinct majority. Sometimes such people wonder if it's worth making such a fuss, and whether anti-Semitic views should really be seen as threatening.

Does "fighting" have to imply a specific activity? In my opinion, a fight is any public opposition or dissent from any free expression of anti-Semitic viewpoints. There are many such anonymous fighters: those who stand up against their families or peers and have the courage to have their own opinion, those who erase hate graffiti from walls and buses. In these ways, many young people say "no."

Groups of anti-racist volunteers monitor the Internet and try to free it of anti-Semitic Web pages. Local representatives of nongovernmental organizations promote multiculturalism and tolerance. Tens of thousands of signatures of school pupils were recently collected in a campaign involving anti-racist, civic, and even ecological organizations against hate speech at sports events. Projects to paint over slogans on walls also involve numerous young people. The most famous of these takes place every year in Lodz, but both smaller and larger cities have already followed this example. Sometimes pupils from all schools in a city set off down the streets carrying paint; sometimes it is only one school or classroom that participates. A high school girl from Wroclaw brought the problem of graffiti on city walls and their hateful content to the attention of the media by preparing an exhibit of documentary photographs of such defacings in her city. This, too, was a fight against anti-Semitism—the brave and outspoken objection of a young girl.

One particularly important method of fighting is education. I can think of many people, organizations, and schools that are involved with conquering prejudice through workshops about culture and tolerance, through getting to know the religious customs of others. An important

---

Previous page: Annual campaign to paint over anti-Semitic graffiti on walls, organized by the City of Lodz Office, with the name of "Colorful Tolerance." Courtesy of the City of Lodz Office

element is meetings between Polish and Jewish youth, which counteract mutual prejudices and stereotypes. This is also a way to fight, though it involves not confronting something bad, but rather strengthening and nurturing something good.

The kinds of initiatives mentioned are numerous, and many young people are involved in them. Of course, not all Polish youth are out fighting anti-Semitism, nor do young people have no prejudices. But there is more and more knowledge about the shared history and culture of Jews and Poles—both moments of beauty and of pain. And there is ever more fondness and understanding.

ZUZANNA RADZIK is a student in theology, involved in Christian-Jewish dialogue, who publishes in Catholic magazines and papers. She wrote the article "Piwnice wciąż gniją" (The Cellars are Still Rotting) in which she described her battle against an anti-Semitic bookshop in Warsaw. She is a member of the board of the Forum for Dialogue Among Nations.

Pupils from the history club of the primary school in Wielowies, near Gliwice, restoring the local Jewish cemetery. Photo by G. Kaminski

DAVID PELEG

▶ 30. What kind of attitudes do Poles have toward the State of Israel?

Poland views its relationship with Israel as unique and strategic. Poles, who have known partitions, loss of national territory, German-Nazi occupation, and Communist regimes, express sympathy and understanding for the political and security situation of Israel, and for the dilemmas facing the government of Israel in trying to promote peace with security.

Poland views its relationship with Israel as unique and strategic. Poles, who have known partitions, loss of national territory, German-Nazi occupation, and Communist regimes, express sympathy and understanding for the political and security situation of Israel, and for the dilemmas facing the government of Israel in trying to promote peace with security.

Poland supports the efforts to achieve peace in the Middle East and is ready to contribute to them. Poland maintains forces in Iraq, which also ensures the security of Israel, and participates in UNIFIL and UNDOF UN peacekeeping operations on Israel's borders with Syria and Lebanon. Both Poland and Israel see their relationship with the United States as strategic and existential and would like to develop an American-Israeli-Polish triangle.

Poland gives high priority to its relations with Israel within Polish foreign policy, and works to develop bilateral relations with Israel in all possible fields.

Politically, Poland wishes to contribute actively within the European Union to a balanced policy toward Israel, to contain Iran's quest for nuclear weapons, and to oppose its calls for the extermination of Israel and denial of the Holocaust. Trade between Poland and Israel is developing, and relationships between the military establishments and the defense industries of the two countries are excellent. Culturally, because of the common history of Poles and Jews, there is wide exchange in the fields of literature, music, theatre, and painting, and the Polish government has planned a season of Polish culture in Israel for 2008.

Before the Second World War 3.5 million Jews lived in Poland (10 percent of the population), but more than three million were murdered by the Nazi-Germans and their collaborators. Most of the killings were done in the death camps built by Nazi Germany on occupied Polish soil, and Poland, with the support of Israel, rejects references to the camps as "Polish camps" as a falsification of history.

←

Previous page: Western wall of the Temple, the so-called Wailing Wall in Jerusalem. Courtesy of Israel's Ministry of Tourism

Next page: Basilica of the Church of the Holy Sepulcher, Jerusalem. Courtesy of Israel's Ministry of Tourism

Poland works to keep alive the memory of the millions of Polish Jews who were murdered, to educate young Poles about what happened during the war, to fight anti-Semitism, and to encourage reconciliation between young Poles and young Israelis. For Poles, it is important to develop the Polish narrative of what happened during the war: the millions of non-Jewish Poles who were murdered by the Germans, including during the Warsaw Uprising; and the thousands of Poles who saved Jews while risking their own lives and the lives of their families and who have been recognized by Israel as righteous persons.

DAVID PELEG is the ambassador of Israel to Poland. Since 1965, he has been working as a diplomat in Africa, America, and Europe. From 1998-2000, he was the permanent representative of Israel to the United Nations in Geneva.

MACIEJ KOZLOWSKI

▶ 31. What do Israelis think about contemporary Poland and Poles?

Many Israelis, tracing their Polish roots, after visiting our country realize that we are a free and democratic state, bearing no resemblance to the one that they or their parents or grandparents recall from the prewar era, the 1950s, or the 1960s.

Just as with all other topics, Israelis think many different things about Poland. Some think well of it, some poorly, and still others don't think about it at all because they know nothing about Poland. Therefore, the question should be framed so as to learn in what proportions these attitudes exist or whether the stance of Israeli citizens toward Poland and Poles is changing, and if so, in which direction?

The question itself is important because the sentiments of Israelis regarding Poland have never been as indifferent as they are to, say, Ireland, Holland or Norway. The vast majority of the founders first of the *yishuv* (the pre-1948 Jewish community in mandate Palestine) and then of the State of Israel were originally from Poland. They arrived in Israel with a culture and worldview formed in Poland, as well as sentiments toward Poland as the country where their ancestors had lived for centuries. But they also often brought with them feelings of prejudice and regret about Poland, a country that had often let them know that they were not at home there.

To such feelings about prewar Poland was added the tragedy of the Shoah. The extermination as a whole was planned and carried out by the Germans, but it took place on Polish ground and Poles were its witnesses. At times they empathized, risking their lives to offer help, but often they were indifferent. And it also happened that at times—however sporadically—Poles actively participated in the extermination.

After the war, following a brief period of close cooperation around the creation of the Polish and Israeli states, Polish-Israeli relations cooled and were finally ruptured, this time at Moscow's prompting. Accompanying this was the disgraceful anti-Semitic campaign of 1968, organized by the Polish Communist state government, animating all the old injuries and grudges. Through an entire generation—twenty-three years—there was not only the absence of any contact between our two countries, but Poland and Poles were presented in Israel in the blackest of hues. When Poland regained its freedom in 1989 and once again entered into relations with Israel, a slow process of making up for years of hostility and resentment began.

So where on this path do we stand at present?

<hr>

Previous page: The Jewish cemetery in Bobowa. Photo by Erica Lehrer
Next page: Skyscrapers in the center of Warsaw. Photo by P. Toczynski/Forum

Much is being done. Many Israelis, tracing their Polish roots, after visiting our country realize that we are a free and democratic state, bearing no resemblance to the one that they or their parents or grandparents recall from the prewar era, the 1950s, or the 1960s. They see that anti-Semitism, while still present, is not a dominant feature in the Polish social landscape, but quite the opposite; there is an active interest in Jewish culture and tradition as a part of our shared history, as well as an interest in contemporary Israel. Moreover, they see that in Poland far more frequently than in other European countries one encounters an understanding of Israel's contemporary struggles. Among people interested in world politics, it is understood that in the international arena Poland takes a more balanced attitude regarding Israeli security than what is typical in other countries.

An enormous role in overcoming the negative image of Poland and Poles was played by Pope John Paul II, who for years strove indefatigably to improve Jewish-Christian relations. The pope's historic visit to Israel in 2000 was a particularly significant step in this process. A real turning point came with the induction of Poland into the European Union. Just before its formal acceptance, interest began in obtaining renewed Polish citizenship and afterwards a veritable avalanche of Israelis declared their desires to apply for it.

Thus a change of attitude toward Poland is occurring. Of course, it is not as fast or as widespread as one might wish. An important role could and should be played through the mass trips of young Israelis to Poland. These should be planned with the condition that young Israelis explore not only places connected to the Holocaust, but present-day Poland and its inhabitants, among whom their ancestors lived and shaped their identities for centuries. Finally, young Israelis must have the opportunity to meet with young Poles of their own generation. Nothing builds connections better than direct, personal contact.

DR. MACIEJ KOZLOWSKI is a historian, diplomat, former ambassador of the Republic of Poland in Israel, and former Polish deputy minister of foreign affairs.

Jewish Presence
in Contemporary Poland

HELENA DATNER

▸ 32. Are there any Jews still living in Poland?

In Poland there are a few thousand Jews. Fewer than 4,000 are registered with Jewish organizations, although new institutions are now being established, and in some of the older ones—for example, in the religious community—the membership is increasing. Besides Jews who are the members of such organizations, there is a significantly larger circle of people of Jewish heritage who are interested in Jewish issues but do not wish to manifest their Jewishness through association with some kind of institution.

This question is frequently asked in a slightly different guise: "How many Jews are there in Poland?" Many people are interested in the answer. In Poland there are a few thousand Jews. Fewer than 4,000 are registered with Jewish organizations, although new institutions are now being established, and in some of the older ones—for example, in the religious community—the membership is increasing. Besides Jews who are the members of such organizations, there is a significantly larger circle of people of Jewish heritage who are interested in Jewish issues but do not wish to manifest their Jewishness through association with some kind of institution. For this group it is difficult not only to establish, but even to estimate the numbers. It is likely there are tens of thousands of such people.

What are Polish Jews like? First, one must recognize that between 1950-89 it was not easy for them to cultivate a Jewish identity. During the period of socialist rule, until the anti-Semitic events of 1968, there was a rather resilient Jewish life, considering the circumstances. That reality should not be undervalued, despite the fact that Jewish life existed in exclusively secular form. After all, one must recall that Polish Jews, in particular, had a rich prewar national tradition based on Yiddish culture, with its own literature, press, theater, and cinema. Today, younger Jews in Poland, for the first time in many years, are beginning to think of their Jewishness in terms of Judaism.

Where did young Polish Jews come from? In the 1970s and '80s it seemed that Jewish life was fading away, and beautiful picture albums appeared, among them *The Last Jews of Poland*. Furthermore, unlike in Germany, where there was a massive increase in the size of the Jewish community due to Russian immigration, immigration was not (and is not) a factor in the number of Jews in Poland.

Many Jews in Poland today have parents who were born before the war and, after managing to survive it, did not leave Poland—some of them simply because they wanted to stay here and build a life within the new political system, which, they believed, would eliminate all discrimination. At that time, for people who had survived the Holocaust, this was a very compelling motivation. It is easy to forget this belief today, knowing as we do that the hopes for solving the problem

←————————————

Previous page: A marriage ceremony of Izrael and Sara Korzonkowski at the Nozyk Synagogue in Warsaw. Photo by B. Zajac

A class in the Jewish school in Warsaw. Photo by E. Serotta

of anti-Semitism through socialism were, in the end, futile. Others, after what they went through during the war, did not want to be Jewish any longer; they preferred to submerge themselves in the surrounding environment, to rid themselves of the stigma of being Jewish, which had led to such terrible suffering. Others stayed for diverse human motivations, among them—despite all they had been through—attachment to Poland, the country of their birth. One's birthplace is a significant personal biographical element—often extremely important—and not easy to forget.

Many Jews in Poland discovered their parents' Jewish backgrounds late in life. In general, their parents did not pass on their Jewish culture to their children, either because they did not want to, or because they did not themselves have much to pass on, and between 1968 and 1989 (when this generation was growing up) Jewish institutions were weak. The social climate in Poland at that time was decidedly unfavorable for seeking one's Jewish roots. The grandchildren's generation,

Next page: A bar mitzvah celebrated by a thirteen-year-old Jewish boy to mark his coming of age and becoming a full member of the community. In the background is Rabbi Michael Schudrich, chief rabbi of Poland, at the Nozyk Synagogue in Warsaw. Photo by Monika Krajewska

growing up after the change in government in 1989, had, and now has, a significantly more conducive environment for such searching. Freedom did away with various social taboos: This is evident in all post-Communist countries. It became much easier to talk about Jews and Judaism, and parents more frequently and more happily now tell their children about their heritage. Freedom also facilitates the establishment or renewal of Jewish institutions, without which Jewish life is impossible.

Sometimes, general questions about Jews living in Poland that appear to be based on simple curiosity conceal other, more freighted questions, such as: How *can* a Jew live in Poland after the Holocaust—in a place that is the cemetery of the Jewish nation? Or, alternatively, how can a Jew live here after 1968? Our Jewish brethren from abroad often ask us these questions.

In brief, Jews who live in Poland are not lunatics. They live here because Poland is their country, because they were born here, just as American Jews feel about the United States or French Jews about France. Today, in any case, with anti-Semitic incidents rising in many countries, the ratings of Poland have improved. This is a small comfort, although one important conclusion can be drawn: Anti-Semitism cannot be blamed on one country. Particular condemnation of Poland misses the point and the truth. Moreover, there is something more important still: One lives in a place because of thousands of ties that bind a person there, for better and for worse. At times, to be sure, it is for worse.

This question is asked by anti-Semites, as well. Sociological research shows that the more one dislikes Jews, the more Jews one thinks there are. This is understandable: After all, someone has to "rule Poland." Jews, according to this obsession, rule Poland, and thus there must really be a lot of them, some hundreds of thousands at minimum. The anti-Semitic personality is, without fail, an obsessive personality. The number of Jews suggested by anti-Semites is ridiculous. The problem is that ridicule, unfortunately, is not a sufficient cure for anti-Semitism.

HELENA DATNER is a sociologist who has carried out research on anti-Semitism in Poland, and who works as a translator. She is a former president of Warsaw's Jewish community.

Konstanty Gebert

▶ 33. Is it dangerous to be a Jew in Poland today?

No. Incidents of anti-Semitic violence are rare. Poland is a safe country for Jews, but it is not, nor can it be, a comfortable one. The weight of history is too great and bloody for us to feel here as we might in any other country.

In recent years the Jewish Historical Institute was pelted with stones, and arson was attempted at the Warsaw and Wroclaw synagogues and the Jewish retreat center in Srodborow near Warsaw. More frequent is harassment of people with identifiably Jewish dress. Generally these are confined to verbal abuse, and inadvertent witnesses typically intervene in an attempt to pacify the attacker. I wear a *kipa* on my head, and I've experienced a few nonthreatening encounters in Warsaw; in Paris, which I visit, attacks are much more frequent, more brutal, and passersby simply avert their gaze.

More pointed attacks have been experienced by Jewish groups, particularly if they make their Jewishness evident. Their mere presence is sometimes taken as a provocation: Attackers are convinced that they are simply responding to a prior taunt, which the sheer presence of Jews on Polish streets amounts to in their eyes. This is evidence, of course, of the existence and potential of latent anti-Semitism, which also manifests itself in widespread anti-Semitic imagery and graffiti. Further, the most recent public opinion polls indicate an increase in anti-Semitic attitudes in Poland during the last ten years (as well as an accompanying rise in anti-anti-Semitic attitudes, which are noticeably more widespread).

Nevertheless, the fact remains that Jewish events and property do not require the extraordinary security measures that are the norm in Western Europe. Only very recently have more frequent police patrols appeared in the area of the synagogue in Warsaw, and prior to religious services a few security guards have been hired by the Jewish community to ensure safety. The Festival of Jewish Culture in Cracow, during which thousands of people assemble on the streets of the historical Jewish Quarter of the city, takes place with the same police presence which is standard for any such big event; no significant incidents have resulted. The last Israeli ambassador, the unusually popular and easily identifiable Shevach Weiss, danced several times there among the crowds without his bodyguard. Public, university-sponsored meetings on Jewish themes, even those relating to the Middle East conflict, in which I often take part, occur without incident, and clear expressions of sympathy for Israel are not met with protest.

←

Previous page: Boys with small Israeli flags during the Warsaw Jewish Community Open Day. Photo by T. Gzell/PAP

Concert in Nowy Square during the Cracow festival of Jewish culture, June 2005. Photo by P. Mazur

Public pro-Palestinian events, as a rule, attract no more than a few dozen people, and they are generally peaceful. Nor do major anti-Semitic or anti-Israel events occur. (On the other hand, in Poland there has thus far not been any significant demonstration against anti-Semitism.)

There are, however, places and environments in Poland where Jews really might be threatened with aggression, although generally only verbally. Lodz, hard hit by economic crisis and unemployment, is the capital of the Polish skinheads, and public symptoms of anti-Semitism occur there significantly more frequently than elsewhere. Oswiecim, a city of a few tens of thousand inhabitants stigmatized by the Auschwitz concentration camp that the Germans created there, has looked with displeasure on the annual visits of the March of the Living, an event organized in such a way as to minimize contact with the local inhabitants of the town. Only in the last few years has the local city government been consulted about the course of the March. Gdansk has its church of Saint Bridget, where until recently priest Henryk Jankowski, infamous for his anti-Semitic appearances, presided.

Sunday masses there would assemble several hundred like-minded people. In this and similar places, recognizably Jewish people would certainly be at risk of taunts.

Broadly speaking, hostility against Jews, when it occurs, is directly proportional to their degree of isolation from the local environment. Traveling groups of foreign Jews, often intentionally avoiding contact with Poles and even demonstrating their reluctance for such contact, are thus the most likely targets. At the same time, however, visiting Jews who attempt to make contact with Poles can expect good will and curiosity. Most Poles have never talked to a Jew, despite the constant presence of Jewish issues in the public arena. Finally, Polish Jews, living as they do in a non-Jewish environment to which they are tied by a thousand bonds, very rarely experience attacks in their homes or workplaces. I have never been attacked on my street or in my milieu—although, of course, the cosmopolitan center of Warsaw cannot be taken as representative of Poland as such.

There is no discrimination against Jews in Polish public life. I know of no example of anyone being turned down for a job or denied a promotion because of his Jewish ancestry, although statistically speaking, such incidents must occur. In response to the experience of the Communist era, during which freedom of speech was strangled, the government does not wish to suppress opinions, even offensive ones like anti-Semitism. Anti-Semitic books and publications exist, and are available from street vendors and in many churches as well as on newsstands. At the same time, however, anti-Semitic content appears exceedingly rarely in mainstream publications—although this has been changing significantly in the last few months. The Middle East conflict is also being covered in a manner noticeably more objective than that found in the press of Western Europe. Visible symptoms of anti-Semitism are publicly condemned by moral, religious, and secular authorities, and often also by politicians.

Not every example of dislike of Jews is necessarily anti-Semitic in character. The participation of Communists of Jewish origin in the repressive Stalinist system remains a very painful memory among Poles, although it is also magnified out of proportion and subjected to demagogical manipulation. So, too, the harmful generalizations about the supposedly innate anti-Semitism of Poles—not uncommonly heard among visiting Jews—provoke equally disproportionate defensive reactions.

Poland is a safe country for Jews, but it is not, nor can it be, a comfortable one. The weight of history is too great and too bloody for us to feel as we might in any other country, regardless of whether we are at home or only visitors. But precisely for this reason, we Jews should be vigilant against looking at Poland through our own, however justified, prejudices.

KONSTANTY GEBERT is a *Gazeta Wyborcza* journalist and writer. In 1997, he founded, and until 2000 was the editor-in-chief of *Midrasz*, a Jewish intellectual monthly. He was a member of the democratic opposition in the Communist Poland. He is the author of four books, including *Dziesięć dni Europy* (Ten Days of Europe), 2004 and *Wojna czterdziestoletnia* (Forty Years' War), 2004.

STANISLAW KRAJEWSKI

▶ 34. Do Gentiles and Jews socialize together in Poland today?

In Poland today, Jews are generally Poles. They are not differentiated by language, culture, or basic knowledge about the world. They live and work among Christian Poles. Only a very few Jews, those who work in Jewish organizations, have everyday contact exclusively or mainly with other Jews.

In Poland today, Jews are generally Poles. They are not differentiated by language, culture, or basic knowledge about the world. They live and work among Christian Poles. Only a very few Jews, those who work in Jewish organizations, have everyday contact exclusively or mainly with other Jews.

Shared work produces closeness, which often leads to social relations. This is especially the case among young people in school, and almost all Jews go to state or private schools, where they are small minorities. Further, even in Jewish schools—of which there are two, one in Warsaw and a smaller one in Wroclaw—not all the students are Jewish. Close contacts and friendships with non-Jews are thus typical for practically all young Polish Jews. Another reason for contacts is that Jews live in cities, often in buildings where their neighbors are non-Jews. In Poland, neighborly relations are quite lively. Visiting one's neighbors is the norm—although perhaps this custom is disappearing among the younger generation.

One might say that working, living, and even going to school together does not necessarily lead to close social relationships. But for today's Polish Jews one can go beyond saying that they live among Poles; as a rule, they also have Christians as members of their own families. Most either come from mixed marriages (Jewish–non-Jewish), or they themselves are married to non-Jewish partners, or they have children who have married Catholics. Not infrequently, all of these circumstances apply. Familial contacts thus naturally occur, and such occasions as weddings and funerals lead to even religious Polish Jews being familiar with the church and Catholic customs.

It is true that people often prefer to associate with those who are similar to themselves, those with shared sensibilities. Jews thus generally have many Jewish acquaintances, and sometimes their friends are mostly Jews. Still, staying within a purely Jewish environment requires unusual effort and an explicit avoidance of others. Jews who live like this are the exception. After all, they read the same newspapers, watch the same television programs, and live with more or less the same concerns as their Christian neighbors. The only exception occurs with an occasional Jew from abroad who lives temporarily in Poland.

In light of the above, it is clear that the question itself indicates a complete lack of understanding of the situation of Polish Jews in con-

---

Previous page: Marking the anniversary of the Lodz Ghetto liquidation.
Courtesy of the City of Lodz Office

temporary Poland. But the question is not simply the result of a misunderstanding: Before World War II, when there existed an enormous Jewish community in Poland, many Jews did *not* have close relations with non-Jews. Even some university graduates had never been guests in a Christian household. Their memories have been passed on to the next generation, and for this reason, the question with which we began does not surprise me. In any case, the present day is another story. In the domain of social life, as in any other domain, the familiar picture from the prewar era has no relevance and only hinders understanding of the current situation.

It is fitting to end on a personal note: I, a Jew, maintain social relations with non-Jewish friends, whom I met during my studies, in the ranks of the political opposition during the Communist period, among mountain-climbing enthusiasts, among parents of handicapped children like my younger son, a Down's syndrome child, and in Catholic intellectual circles (among others, my friends from the Council of Christians and Jews).

DR. STANISLAW KRAJEWSKI is a logician and writer. He works in the Institute of Philosophy at Warsaw University. He is the author of books and articles in the discipline of logic, the philosophy of mathematics, Jewish culture and religion, and interreligious dialogue. He is co-chairman of the Polish Council of Christians and Jews, a member of the International Auschwitz Council, and the representative in Poland of the American Jewish Committee.

Members of the Polish Council of Christians and Jews during the March of Remembrance and Prayer in the Warsaw Ghetto. Photo by Monika Krajewska

Stanislaw Krajewski

▶ 35. Do Jews want to retrieve their properties in Poland?

The most straightforward answer is, in general, yes, just like all former property owners and their heirs. A question thus formulated assumes that the question of property restitution—or reprivatization (not to be confused with privatization)—is somehow uniquely a Jewish one. Nothing of the sort: This problem concerns all former owners—as much individuals as institutions.

Szeroka Street in the Jewish district of Cracow called Kazimierz.
Photo by L. Filak

The most straightforward answer is, in general, yes, just like all former property owners and their heirs. A question thus formulated assumes that the question of property restitution—or reprivatization (not to be confused with privatization)—is somehow uniquely a Jewish one. Nothing of the sort: This problem concerns all former owners—as much individuals as institutions. Paradoxically, the interests and attitudes of the Polish community in the United States in this sphere are identical with the interests and attitudes of American Jews, and yet, like so many issues concerning Poland, there is both a difference of opinion and tension between the two communities.

That Polish property reclaimed by Jews is treated as something peculiar, indeed as something particularly suspicious, reveals a problem. Clearly, some think that Jews are not entitled to equal rights.

Previous page: The Old Synagogue in Cracow. Photo by L. Filak

Jewish Meisels Street, a street bustling with life, situated in the Kazimierz district in Cracow, before World War II. Courtesy of the Jewish Historical Institute

One should take into account that the vast majority of Polish Jews were murdered during the German occupation. The Germans plundered a portion of their victims' property, but much remained—thus the emergence today of property and objects without owners or heirs. These properties were taken over, in part, by neighbors and, in part, by local governments or the Polish state, and managed by Communists as "unclaimed" or "abandoned" property. This abuse constituted merely a fragment of the overall policy of the Communist government. Because many decades have passed since that time, there is no good, simple way out. It is not clear who has the strongest claim to Jewish property for which heirs cannot be found—Jewish institutions in Poland (despite the fact that there are very few Jews in Poland today) or international Jewish institutions (although they are not directly connected to Poland) or Israel (although it is a separate country).

I once proposed that Jews pledge to abandon the question of heirless property in exchange for a promise by the Polish government to

Deteriorating house in the Jewish district of Kazimierz in Cracow.
Photo by L. Filak

finance a great museum of the history of Polish Jewry. Unfortunately, there is no one on the Jewish side to partner with the government in such an endeavor. Regardless of one's personal opinion about the problem of heirless property, a solution needs to be found concerning property whose owner or inheritor *can* be identified.

It is necessary to distinguish between two issues: the restitution of Jewish religious-communal property, and reprivatization, or the return of property to private owners. Jewish religious communities are in the process of reclaiming "religious" property, mainly synagogues, schools, and cemeteries, through the proceedings of a commission jointly appointed by the Ministry of Domestic Affairs and the Association of Jewish Religious Communities in Poland. The restitution is taking place on the basis of a 1997 law pertaining to the relations of the Polish state to Polish Jewish communities. It is entirely analogous to statutes regarding the Catholic Church and other churches, which also deal with the problem of restitution. Reclamation of property is occurring, but there are problems with its slow tempo and the difficulties commonly encountered on the local governmental level. The buildings reclaimed are ruins as well as valuable property. There is hope that the efforts of the Jewish community will facilitate restoration, and yet even the most successful restitution will hardly suffice for the timely protection of more than a thousand Jewish cemeteries, which, according to Jewish law, should remain undisturbed in perpetuity.

The return of private property is not legally regulated. Numerous owners—of course, not only Jews—in and outside of Poland are awaiting such regulation. Dozens of attempts, undertaken since 1989, have not produced results. Poland is the only country in this part of Europe where the issue still remains open. The longer it drags on, the more difficult it is to achieve closure. In the meantime, investigations regarding property are being brought to various courts. This is possible in cases where one can argue that the dispossession of the property during the postwar era involved the violation of the laws in force at that time. But some kind of global settlement is needed. Even a partial solution would make sense, as long as it would not discriminate against anyone. Some previous attempts were discriminatory in character because they tried to exclude people who are not Polish citizens. Clearly at issue was the specific exclusion of Jews—and Jews will not agree to this.

DR. STANISLAW KRAJEWSKI is a logician and writer. He works in the Institute of Philosophy at Warsaw University. He is the author of books and articles in the discipline of logic, the philosophy of mathematics, Jewish culture and religion, and interreligious dialogue. He is co-chairman of the Polish Council of Christians and Jews, a member of the International Auschwitz Council, and the representative in Poland of the American Jewish Committee.

MICHAL BILEWICZ

▸ 36. Are Jews loyal to the countries they live in or to Israel?

Allegations of Jewish disloyalty to the state are some of the most common accusations that Polish Jews have heard from their compatriots. In our country Jews have been frequently accused of excessive sympathy to the czar, later to the Soviet government, and finally to Israel.

Allegations of Jewish disloyalty to the state are some of the most common accusations that Polish Jews have heard from their compatriots. In our country Jews have been frequently accused of excessive sympathy to the czar, later to the Soviet government, and finally to Israel. In turn, an opinion poll recently carried out in five European Union countries showed that as many as 56 percent of Europeans think that Jews are more loyal to Israel than to the countries in which they live. It is worth asking oneself what these accusations are based on: Is there a kernel of truth in them, or are they pure slander?

The sympathy of the majority of European Jews with Israel is a fact, and an unsurprising one. Among the founders of the Jewish state in the Middle East were many Jews from Eastern Europe. Of the eight first prime ministers of the State of Israel (that is, until 1996), only one was not born on the terrain of today's Poland, Russia, Belorussia or the Ukraine. Recall that many Jews from this region emigrated to Israel as a safe haven after the Holocaust, postwar pogroms, or the anti-Semitic purge of 1968. For thousands of Jews from the poverty-stricken cities of Russia and Ukraine, Israel offered a new home in which they could live and work with dignity. As a result, today almost every Pole, Russian, or European with Jewish ancestry has a relative—parents, cousins, far-removed aunts, or grandparents—living in Israel. And to their fate—the fate of our families—we are not indifferent.

After the atrocities of World War II, the existence of a Jewish state in Israel became a guarantee for those Jews who feared that the Holocaust might be repeated at any time. Even today, in fact, in Europe and in Poland neo-fascist groups exist, and more than one politician has made a career using anti-Semitic slogans. We must remember that the plan to annihilate European Jewry came about in a highly developed country that constituted the avant-guard of European culture, and that the party responsible for the Holocaust was voted in on the basis of fully democratic procedures. Thus, for many Jews, the existence of a strong Israel is a guarantee of security, a life-preserver for the entire Jewish Diaspora.

The establishment of the State of Israel was received particularly enthusiastically by Jews in Communist countries. When the last inde-

---

Previous page: Members of the Polish Union of Jewish Students during the March of the Living in Oswiecim. Photo by P. Turecki

Grandfather with his grandson reading *With Fire and Sword* (a patriotic novel set in the time of war between seventeenth-century Poland and Ukraine) by Henryk Sienkiewicz in Yiddish, prewar Warsaw. Courtesy of the Jewish Historical Institute

pendent Jewish organizations were made illegal in the Polish People's Republic and the Soviet Union, and Jewish writers and political party activists were thrown into jail, Israel appeared as a distant enclave of freedom. Therefore, when Golda Meir came to Moscow in 1948, 40,000 Soviet Jews came to hear her at the last functioning synagogue in the city, and the meeting evolved into a giant demonstration of solidarity with Israel. Later, many Russian refuseniks were thrown in jail for sympathizing with the Jewish state.

Although Jewish supporters of a strong Israel are numerous, it must be noted that some of the most vocal critics of Israel are Jewish as well. Jewish political writers and journalists like Norman Finkelstein, Michael Warschawski, and Uri Avnery, and even Orthodox rabbis associated with Neturei Karta are highly critical of Israeli politics. And if we could point to one group as, in some sense of the word, the most devoted to Israel, it would not be Jews, but rather evangelical Christians, who, for their own religious reasons stake out radically pro-Israel positions.

Nevertheless, it is true that many Diaspora Jews try to influence the politics of their countries toward a pro-Israel stance. Arabs apply similar pressures in European countries for a pro-Arab or pro-Palestinian stance, yet they are rarely accused of disloyalty. What's more, no one is surprised that women's organizations tried to persuade their governments to support the war against the Taliban or to put pressure on Iran, in the interest of women's rights. Did anyone say that women were thereby bad citizens of their countries?

Poland's incorporation into NATO came to pass, in large part, thanks to the Polish diaspora in the United States calling on the American Senate to support the move. It is important to understand that Jewish sympathy for Israel does not distinguish Jews from other interest groups, from Buddhists defending Tibet, women fighting against the Taliban, or ecologists protesting the cutting down of forests in Brazil—members of these groups have the right to express their aspirations in a democratic society. Such activities make them better, not worse, citizens of their countries.

MICHAL BILEWICZ is a social psychologist, Ph.D. candidate in the Department of Psychology at Warsaw University, and a former journalist for *Slowo Zydowskie* **(Jewish Word). He is former editor-in-chief of** *Jidele,* **a magazine for Jewish youth. Presently he is vice-president of the Forum for Dialogue Among Nations.**

Konstanty Gebert

▶ 37. How can Jews live in the country where their ancestors were murdered?

Poland is an exceptional country: The Shoah was carried out here. If it had been carried out at the initiative of Poles, or with Polish support, that would be a sufficient argument for not living here. But the Germans chose Poland to be the site of their crimes, not because it was populated by Poles, but rather because it was populated by Jews. The factories of death were, quite logically, in the place where their intended victims were located.

This is clearly not a question for Poland alone, but could be posed to Jews living today in any part of Eastern Europe occupied by the Germans during World War II. There is no place on our continent where Jews did not experience persecution and violent bloodshed. Does this mean we should abandon Europe? From the classical Zionist perspective, perhaps, yes. However, while we support those among us who move to Israel, just as we support the Jewish state, simply put, I don't need a rally call from Israel urging me to get out of Poland; for that, local anti-Semites will suffice. But ideological issues aside, perhaps it would just be sensible to move elsewhere, to a safe country whose history is not drenched in Jewish blood, where Jewish life is easy and straightforward—e.g., to the U.S. Again, we are happy when one of us manages to settle across the ocean and avails himself of all the benefits that life there offers, but we don't believe we should all follow suit.

This simple response could be given by Jews from any European country, but Poland is an exceptional country: The Shoah was carried out here. If it had been carried out at the initiative of Poles, or with Polish support, that would be a sufficient argument for not living here. But the Germans chose Poland to be the site of their crimes, not because it was populated by Poles, but rather because it was populated by Jews. Half of the victims of the Shoah were Polish Jews. The factories of death were located, quite logically, where their intended victims were.

Of course, it is also true that had the Germans wanted Polish aid for their crimes, possibly they would have received it. There is no reason to assume that the Poles would have acted differently from, say, the French or the Ukrainians. Testimony to this conclusion can be found in the distinct indifference to the fate of the Jews on the part of the majority of Poles during the occupation, and the active participation in the Shoah of a difficult-to-estimate, yet visible, part of Polish society, from blackmailers to murderers. Their crimes, however, are a stain on the history of the Poles—but not of Poland. The Nazis hated Poland too much to want to collaborate with it, and they killed too

---

Previous page: Tablets with names of the victims murdered in the death camp of Belzec. Photo by E. Serotta

Panorama of the "Osiedle za Zelazna Brama" estate in Warsaw, the part of the northern district inhabited mostly by the Jews before World War II. During the Second World War it was the ghetto district. Currently many Jews live here to be in the vicinity of the only synagogue in Warsaw. Photo by A. Kondrat

many Poles for collaboration to be possible: Of the six million Polish citizens murdered during the war, Jews made up one half; ethnic Poles made up the other.

The Polish government-in-exile was the first to alert the world to the Nazi genocide, and they were the first to condemn it. And these were not merely words. It is difficult to count not only the criminal accomplices, but also those who secretly saved Jews, risking their lives, and often paying with their lives. This is how my grandfather survived: To save him, the help of more than ten righteous people was required, the number for whom the Lord spared Sodom. I won't be more demanding than God, all the more so because those saved were in the tens of thousands. The greatest number of trees in the Forest of the Righteous at Yad Vashem in Jerusalem carry Polish surnames, each representing a rescuer of Jews who answered both the calls of conscience and the appeals of the Polish underground.

Again it is true that Polish rescuers had to guard more vigilantly against their own countrymen who wanted to turn Jews in than they did against the Germans. But if I were to conclude that Jews shouldn't live in Poland, this would mean aligning with those who claim that, similarly, it was in the Polish interest for Hitler to "solve the Jewish question." I stand in favor of the rescuers and against the blackmailers. The latter betrayed both Jews and Poland.

In any case, the history of anti-Semitism in Poland, as in the rest of Europe, did not begin with the German occupation, nor did it end there. Likewise, the history of the fight against anti-Semitism, as well as against all forms of prejudice, foreign rule, and native dictatorship, also did not begin there. Polish Jews had taken part in that struggle, including its last chapter, which had led to the fall of Communism in 1989. This is our indelible contribution to Poland as Jews: from synagogues and the writings of learned commentators, to factories and hospitals, to scholars in Polish schools and activists in the Polish underground. I refuse to accept a vision of Jewish history in Poland in which only our victimhood is important. My ancestors had lived here for ages and, just as much as the Poles, had helped make this country. I do not intend to turn my back on them, nor their legacy. Finally, most of the people I love are here. I am an unenthusiastic patriot of crests, borders, and banners, whatever kind they may be, but I am a devoted patriot of people. And I am happy that during my life I have had the chance to put my patriotism to a practical test. I won't abandon a country where people went to prison for printing what I wrote.

I also won't abandon other Jews. Those of us who are the best candidates for immigration are often also those who have been able to preserve or reconstruct fuller Jewish identities. The departure of such people would mean that those left behind would be in an even more difficult position to preserve their ties with Judaism—and we should help in the reconstruction of these bonds, not hinder them. This has more than just local significance. Poland is important for Jews around the world, and if not for the Jews of Poland, the others would have a difficult time understanding why.

None of this means that I think that we are all obliged to stay in Poland. The world has become open, and it is difficult for me to foresee even where my children will live ten years from now, but I would not like someone else to tell them where they should or should not live.

KONSTANTY GEBERT is a *Gazeta Wyborcza* journalist and writer. In 1997, he founded, and until 2000 was the editor-in-chief of *Midrasz*, a Jewish intellectual monthly. He was a member of the democratic opposition in the Communist Poland. He is the author of four books, including *Dziesięć dni Europy* (Ten Days of Europe), 2004, and *Wojna czterdziestoletnia* (Forty Years' War), 2004.

Present-Day Israel

Shlomo Avineri

▶ 38. What is the background of the intense Israeli-Palestinian conflict?

The Israeli-Palestinian conflict is a conflict between two national movements. It is a conflict between the Jewish national movement—Zionism—and the Palestinian Arab national movement, and as such, is similar to other national conflicts, like those between Greeks and Turks on Cyprus; Serbs and Albanians in Kosovo; also former conflicts between Poles and Germans, Germans and French, Poles and Ukrainians.

The Israeli-Palestinian conflict is a conflict between two national movements. It is a conflict between the Jewish national movement—Zionism—and the Palestinian Arab national movement, and as such, is similar to other national conflicts, like those between Greeks and Turks on Cyprus; Serbs and Albanians in Kosovo; Serbs, Croats and Muslims in Bosnia; also former conflicts between Poles and Germans, Germans and French, Poles and Ukrainians. As we know from history as well as contemporary politics, such conflicts are often extremely harsh and can be accompanied by cruelty and bitterness that are remembered for generations.

Yet the Israeli-Palestinian conflict has some unique features that are responsible for some aspects of its intensity. It is not a conflict just over borders, as is the case in most national conflicts—it goes deeper: Both sides view the whole territory under question as part of their respective homeland.

For the Jews, this is *Eretz Israel*, the Land of Israel, the Holy Land, the homeland of the Jewish people since circa 1000 B.C.E.; the land of historical memory and glory in the past, the focus of centuries-old dreams of return and redemption. For the Arabs, this is *Filistin*, Palestine, part of the great Arab homeland, stretching from Morocco to Iraq, and as much part of the Arab patrimony as Egypt, Syria or Yemen. It is these conflicting claims that give the conflict its acrimony.

It is clear that in such a case, the only reasonable solution is a compromise. This is what the United Nations suggested in 1947, when the future of the territory, which had been administered by Great Britain since World War I, came before it (earlier, it had been part of the Turkish Empire). The UN realized that both national movements had a claim, yet none of the two claims could be satisfied in their entirety. Hence the UN decided in 1947 to partition British Palestine into two states—a Jewish and an Arab state—allocating to the Jewish state those areas in which there was a Jewish majority and to the Arab state those areas in which there was an Arab majority.

It is the contrasting responses to the UN decision that are at the root of the present conflict. The Jews in Palestine, as well as most Jews outside it, accepted—though with a heavy heart—the compro-

Map of Israel.

Police woman comforting a displaced young Jewish settler. epa/PAP

mise solution offered. While they thought that they had a claim to the whole territory, they realized, both on moral and pragmatic grounds, that only a compromise would be acceptable and feasible. On the other hand, the Arabs—not only those living in Palestine, but also the neighboring Arab states (Egypt, Syria, Iraq, Lebanon)—rejected the UN-sponsored compromise and went to war against the UN resolution and the Jewish community. Palestinian Arabs started terror attacks against Jewish cities and villages, and on termination of British rule on May 15, 1948, the armies of the four Arab neighboring states invaded Israel with the aim of destroying the nascent Jewish state. In the ensuing war, which Israel won, many Arabs fled their homes; some were expelled, and became refugees.

Had the Arabs of Palestine and the neighboring Arab states accepted the UN plan for partition, two states—a Jewish and an Arab—would have been established in 1948; Palestine would now have been independent—alongside Israel—for almost sixty years; there would be no Palestinian refugees, no further wars, no Palestinian terrorism, no Israeli retaliations.

For more than fifty years, Palestinian refugees were kept—by their own leadership—in camps, so as not to give up their claim to return to areas that are part of Israel. Since the Six-Day War of 1967, Israel has also been in control of the West Bank and Gaza, where most Palestinians live. Yet for more than forty years, no Arab country, and no Arab leader was ready to accept Israel's legitimacy and negotiate with it. Both the Arab refusal to accept Israel and the Israeli occupation of the West Bank and Gaza have further deepened the conflict.

In 1977 the first Arab leader to seek an end to the hostilities, President Anwar Sadat of Egypt, traveled to Jerusalem and publicly announced to the Knesset (Parliament) that he was ready to accept Israel and live in peace with it. A peace treaty between Israel and Egypt was signed, in which Israel returned to Egypt the territory of Sinai, occupied by Israel since 1967. A similar peace treaty was signed with Jordan in 1994. Tentative agreements were signed between Israel and the Palestine Liberation Organization in 1993, and a provisional Palestinian Authority has been established in the West Bank and Gaza. Yet it is not yet clear whether the Palestinians are ready to accept the legitimacy of Israel's existence and to come to terms with the fact that

Young Palestinian boy. Photo by C. Fissel

the 1947-48 Palestinian refugees (like Germans who left Polish territories in 1945) will not be able to return.

In summer 2005 Israel implemented a decision—over strong internal dissent—to withdraw from the Gaza Strip and dismantle Jewish settlements there. But real peace in the region will arrive only when it becomes clear that the Palestinians are ready to accept Israel's legitimacy and to live in peace with it. The two-state solution—proposed by the UN in 1947, and at that time rejected by the Arab side—is still the only way to reconciliation and coexistence between Jews and Arabs.

SHLOMO AVINERI, born in Poland, is a professor of political science at the Hebrew University of Jerusalem. He has been a lecturer at the universities of Oxford, Yale, and New York. From 1975-77, he was the director-general of Israel's Ministry of Foreign Affairs. He is the author of *Israel and the Palestinians, Marx's Socialism* and *Hegel's Theory of the Modern State*.

NILI COHEN

▶ 39. Are human rights respected in Israel?

The court faces a difficult dilemma in balancing
security needs with the rights of the individual
in cases of a so-called "ticking bomb." These cases
occur if a bomb is about to explode, causing
damage to life and limb, and the only way to find
and detonate it is to interrogate the person who
set it or knows how to defuse it.

Globalization is associated nowadays not only with information, knowledge, commerce, communications, and law, but also with other aspects much less pleasant that threaten the well-being of the world. These concern crime and terror. The most conspicuous example was the tragedy of 9/11, which changed the history of the world. Many questions were asked in the wake of this devastating event; one concerned the tension between the war against terror and the preservation of human rights.

Unfortunately, this was not a novel issue for Israel. What characterizes both the United States and Israel is the democratic nature of both states. The fight against terror in a dictatorship does not cause much of a dilemma. The basic principles of democracy are a separation of powers and preservation of human rights. Human rights consist mainly of entitlements to private property, freedom of movement, freedom of expression, and due process. In a dictatorship these cherished freedoms and rights are not sacred at all, and no checks and balances can mitigate the abuse of power by the ruler. Therefore, at the slightest suspicion, citizens can be put into jail, tortured, and held without a trial or other guarantees of due process. When acts of terror occur in a dictatorship, the war against the perpetrators would not be coupled with any dilemma regarding guaranteeing the individual's rights, which do not prevail, anyhow.

In short, in a democracy, terror-acts are likely to be more frequent because terrorists exploit the freedom offered by democracy. In a democracy, the answer to the question of how to eliminate terror or reduce its occurrence seems to be quite complicated.

It should be noted that what distinguishes the war against terror from a regular war is reflected in three basic aspects: **participants, time,** and **space**.

Participants: Under international law, war is an act between states. This is altogether different with regard to terror, where not always is it possible to identify a terrorist with a state. Also, the participants in a conventional war are soldiers. In a terror attack, the terrorist would likely try to hide himself, dressing up intentionally as

---

Previous page: Demonstration by Jewish citizens of Israel calling upon their leaders to make peace with the Palestinians.

a civilian. Furthermore, generally in a conventional war, soldiers fight against soldiers. In terror, the target is innocent civilians.

Time: A conventional war is limited in time. There is a declaration of war and, generally, a formal announcement of a truce. A terror attack is timeless. It might exist forever.

Space: A conventional war takes place in a defined territory. A terror attack has no limited space. It might occur anywhere.

To sum up, the laws of war (which apply when a state of war exists) and the law governing the conduct of the war embodied in the Geneva Convention reflect the terrible experience of the First and Second World Wars. These laws did not anticipate the new war on terror and, consequently, do not fit well into the conditions of such a war.

Israel has been facing the problem of terror for many years within its borders and abroad, but the situation in Israel is different from the one prevailing in the United States or Europe. The terrorist threat has always been much more severe in scale and scope. The situation in Israel might be termed a hybrid situation of war: It is not a terror attack as described previously because it is more related to territory and has the character of a fight between states, yet it is not a full-scale war. The Israeli Supreme Court regards the situation as an armed conflict, short of war.

Israel has created some local legal provisions that apply to certain aspects of the situation; for example, recently the Knesset enacted a law that empowers the detention of illegal combatants. Under this law, some Hezbollah terrorists from Lebanon who masterminded terror attacks against Israel are being administratively detained (with a court approval) in Israeli prisons. It is worth noting that the Israeli Supreme Court ruled that these detainees could be incarcerated only if they were threatening to Israel's security. They cannot be kept in prison as bargaining chips. Therefore, the court released some detainees who were judged to be merely bargaining chips.

Besides this particular statute regarding illegal combatants, in many other respects, regular criminal law governs. And it is the Israeli judiciary that has the power to review military actions and must attempt to strike the balance in these difficult times between security needs and individual human rights.

Previous page: Palestinian boy and Israeli soldier. Photo by C. Fissel

Scene from the Palestinian territories. epa/Forum

The Israeli Supreme Court plays a major role in enforcing law, not only in Israel, but also in the West Bank, which is governed by the local law of the territories and by the principles of international law. The fact that there is court scrutiny on military actions and operations in the West Bank is in itself a deterrent factor that operates to protect the rights of the Palestinians in the territories and also enables some negotiations with the army. Hence the Supreme Court (sitting as a court of first appeal) has interfered in some cases of house demolitions: Where it has found the family guilty of abetting terrorism, it has approved the demolitions.

Also, in cases of assigned residence, where, for security reasons, a military commander wishes to remove somebody linked to a terror attack from one place to another, the court must approve, and can do so only after scrutinizing the facts of the case.

The court faces a difficult dilemma in balancing security needs with the rights of the individual in cases of a so-called "ticking bomb." These cases occur if a bomb is about to explode, causing damage to life and limb, and the only way to find and detonate it is to interrogate the person who set it or knows how to defuse it. Using some unpleasant methods of interrogation in this case may be the only way to extract the necessary information. The case presents a moral dilemma:

whether to sacrifice the human dignity, maybe even the well-being, of the detainee, in order to save the actual lives of many innocent people.

The court may be called on after the fact to examine whether the defense of necessity should have applied. This is usually done through an action filed by the detainee or his family claiming that he was illegally interrogated. If the person happens to have had information regarding a ticking bomb, and a violent interrogation saved the life of innocent people, the court would recognize in such cases the defense of necessity. But if, after scrutinizing the case, the court is not convinced that there was real necessity to use force, it might impose criminal or civil sanctions on the security officers who employed illegal methods of interrogation. This serves as an effective deterrent without sacrificing security needs.

An old Latin maxim says *"inter arma enim silent leges,"* which means that during war the laws are silent. The Israeli Supreme Court has rejected this maxim. In my view, the Israeli Supreme Court could serve as a model for the functioning of courts in a time of emergency. Unlike the goddess of justice, who is described as blindfolded, the court is neither blind to the needs of security, nor blind to the rights of the individual.

PROF. NILI COHEN is a member of the Israeli Academy of Science and Humanities and holds the Benno Gitter Chair in Comparative Contract Law at the Faculty of Law of Tel Aviv University. She served as vice-rector (1994-97), and subsequently as rector of this university. Her research interests are contracts, restitution, and comparative law. She is the author of such books as *Contracts, Interference with Contractual Relations* and *Inducing Breach of Contract.*

ROMAN FRISTER

▶ 40. Why has the Israeli army shelled districts where Palestinian civilians live?

Hiding behind the uninvolved civilian population is a long-standing tactic of the Palestinian terrorist organizations, which achieves two goals at once: On the one hand, it ensures relative protection for the terrorists from Israeli retaliation, and on the other, any retaliation aimed at a civilian population produces negative world public opinion responses and serves the propaganda purposes of Islamic fundamentalists.

Inside of a bombarded Palestinian house. epa/Forum

For many months, terrorists of Hamas, Islamic Jihad, and, until the death of Yasir Arafat, the fighters of his own party, Fatah, have shelled both the Israeli town of S'derot and a number of the now-evacuated Jewish settlements in the Gaza Strip with short-range "Kassam" rockets. Dozens of civilians were injured, and some were killed, in the attacks. The attacks on S'derot have continued under the current Hamas government.

The Palestinian rocket launchers have often been placed in thickly populated areas. Rocket production workshops, weapons arsenals, and terrorist hideouts are regularly located in homes and apartments. Underground tunnels, through which explosives are smuggled in from Egypt, have their entries and exits in the basements or ground-floor apartments of inhabitants of the Gaza Strip—often against their will, or with agreement to such dealings made out of fear of the armed fighters of the terrorist organizations. Not long ago we were witness to

Previous page: Demonstration by Palestinians against the Israeli army. epa/Forum

A terrorist explosion in Jerusalem, in which a bomb was planted on a bus.
Courtesy of Embassy of Israel in Warsaw

a demonstration in which Palestinian inhabitants of a border village protested against being used as a "protective shield" for Hamas.

Hiding behind the uninvolved civilian population is a long-standing tactic of the Palestinian terrorist organizations, which achieves two goals at once: On the one hand, it ensures relative protection for the terrorists from Israeli retaliation, and on the other, any retaliation aimed at a civilian population produces negative world public opinion responses and serves the propaganda purposes of Islamic fundamentalists.

This drama long ago became the principal fodder of the mass media, particularly television. Israeli helicopters on the roofs of miserable hovels in the refugee camps or tanks and bulldozers demolishing inhabited settlements appeal strongly to the human imagination and nearly always trigger a negative reaction. We subconsciously identify with those wronged without discerning the crux of the problem. We rarely consider which came first: the chicken or the egg?

It is not Israel that chose the thickly settled areas as battlefields. The terrorists did. They did so with a clear understanding of the consequences. If the leadership of the Israeli army is forced to choose between the murder of an Israeli and the murder of a Palestinian, it will choose the latter option. No country would do otherwise. "We don't accept being shot at like ducks just because someone is doing it from behind the back of a neighbor," said Major General Moshe Kaplinski, deputy chief of the General Staff of the Israel Defense Forces. This declaration perfectly states the essence of the problem.

In the heat of battle, Israeli soldiers may sometimes lose a sense of the boundary between essential and excessive reaction. It happens, then, that the retaliation may be disproportional to the attack. Nevertheless, we cannot forget that too many shots come from around corners, that Israeli soldiers often die because someone else pulled the trigger faster. Feelings of vengeance and fear for one's own life easily become entangled. While such reactions may be difficult to justify, it is entirely possible to comprehend, particularly for anyone who has been in combat.

ROMAN FRISTER, born in Poland, is a writer and journalist living in Israel. He is the director of the Koteret School of Journalism and Communication in Tel Aviv, and a correspondent for the Polish weekly *Polityka* (Politics). He is the author of such books as *The Cap: The Price of a Life* and *Impossible Love*.

ROMAN FRISTER

▶ 41. Why is Israel building a "wall"?

Simply put, the "wall"—in reality, a security barrier that is a fence in many more areas than it is a wall—is there to protect the lives of Israeli citizens. Where the wall separates Palestinian territory from Israeli territory, there has been a significant decrease in the number of infiltrations by armed terrorists and suicide bombers.

Simply put, the "wall"—in reality, a security barrier that is a fence in many more areas than it is a wall—is there to protect the lives of Israeli citizens. Where the wall separates Palestinian territory from Israeli territory, there has been a significant decrease in the number of infiltrations by armed terrorists and suicide bombers. The barrier works primarily because it is supported by an electronic early-warning system.

The International Court of Justice in The Hague regards the building of the wall as contradictory to the demands of international law. It is ironic that the leading figure among this tribunal's judges is a citizen of the country that was the first in history to cut itself off from the world by means of a defensive wall: China.

Like many other of its rulings and resolutions, this verdict of the Hague tribunal has, in the past year, been covered by dust. The United Nations does not recognize it as binding, requiring it to take any concrete actions. The verdict was arrived at, above all, as a political act in support of the Palestinians.

There is no doubt that the barrier inhibits not only the actions of terrorists, but also the everyday existence of Palestinians. In some cases, it separates farmers from their fields; in others, it requires children to wait for crossing points to open to get to school. The Israeli Supreme Court has heard a number of cases involving complaints by such victims, and has repeatedly, in cases where changes could be without sacrificing security, required the military authorities to move the course of the wall—at considerable cost to the Israeli government. This has brought a certain relief, although it has not solved the problem, which is, fundamentally, more political than humanitarian. The wall is not being erected exactly along the pre-1967 borders of the state, which were, in fact, simply the armistice lines that came about at the end of the 1948-49 War of Independence. In some sections it encroaches into the territory of the West Bank. The Palestinians suspect that this is a unilateral attempt by Israel to redraw the border between Israel and

---

Previous page: The steel fence near Har Homa and Beit Sahour, separating Israel from the Palestinian territory.
epa/PAP

Next page: A security barrier separating Israeli land from Palestinian land, Qalqilya, 2005. Reuters/Forum

Palestine; but the line of the wall can be changed later, while the lives of terrorist victims cannot be restored.

This rationale for the wall is fully confirmed by the declaration of the Kadima Party, which won the latest elections. One of the top political priorities of the new prime minister, Ehud Olmert, is to evacuate 70 settlements on the West Bank, as well as to withdraw partially from the occupied areas behind the wall, which—as he announced publicly—will in the future be the border of the State of Israel. This move would assure a Jewish majority within the state, leaving most Palestinians east of the wall. It seems that the new government is determined to carry out this project, although it is doubtful that "the borders of Ehud Olmert" will be approved by the Palestinians (who demand a withdrawal to the border that existed prior to June 1967) or blessed by the European Union, the United Nations, or the United States.

Essentially, independent of its defensive function, the wall is primarily a physical and political expression of a mutual lack of trust between Palestinians and Israelis; it represents part of a psychological wall that divides the two nations. No one can foresee when the barrier will become unnecessary, when peace will come.

ROMAN FRISTER, born in Poland, is a writer and journalist living in Israel. He is the director of the Koteret School of Journalism and Communication in Tel Aviv, and a correspondent for the Polish weekly *Polityka* (Politics). He is the author of such books as *The Cap: The Price of a Life* and *Impossible Love*.

Andrew Baker

▸ 42. What is the difference between criticizing Israel and being anti-Semitic?

Throughout its history, Israel has often confronted political and diplomatic efforts to isolate it and depict it in negative terms. In such cases, where it is demonized or its legitimacy as a state is questioned or it is otherwise held to double standards applied to no other country, these manifestations are a form of anti-Semitism.

Traditional expressions of anti-Semitism have often drawn on myths, stereotypes, and conspiracy theories involving both individual Jews and the Jewish community. The nefarious forgery of czarist Russia, *The Protocols of the Elders of Zion*, described a worldwide Jewish cabal intent on international power and domination. Charges of the blood libel echoed through medieval Europe, with claims that Jews were responsible for the murder of Christian children, whose blood was needed for the preparation of Passover matzos. Church teachings that held Jews liable for the death of Jesus and portrayed Judaism as an errant faith contributed to the negative image of Jews and served as justification for their mistreatment. These anti-Semitic expressions culminated in the genocidal policies of Nazi Germany.

In post-Holocaust Europe, following the death of six million Jews and the destruction of centuries-old Jewish communities, anti-Semitic voices were muted. Some Holocaust survivors returned to their homes, but most built new lives in America or in Israel. The Jewish state, established by a vote of the United Nations, declared its independence in 1948. Israel was both the fulfillment of the Zionist dream to re-establish a Jewish nation in its historic homeland and the acknowledgment of the need for a permanent refuge in the face of harsh historical realities. Since its beginning, Israel has been a nation of refugees, providing a home for Holocaust survivors, for Jews from Arab lands, for Jews from Ethiopia, and for Jews from the former Soviet Union.

And since its beginning, Israel has also been a target. While its legitimacy was established by the United Nations, it was still forced to fight for its life against the combined armies of surrounding Arab countries. Throughout its history, it has often confronted political and diplomatic efforts to isolate it and depict it in negative terms. Although it was later rescinded, the Soviet Union and its satellite states together with the Arab bloc at the United Nations managed to pass the infamous "Zionism is racism" resolution. Throughout the Cold War, anti-Zionism was often employed by Communist nations to single out both Israel and individual Jews for special persecution. Such was the

---

Previous page: Poster in a street in Warsaw with the inscription: "Don't be indifferent towards the death of Palestinians. Stop Sharon the murderer." Photo by R. Szuchta

Demonstration against Israeli policy in front of the Israeli Embassy in Warsaw.
Inscription on the banner: "End Israeli apartheid. One state of equal nations."
Photo by T. Gzell/PAP

case in Poland, for example, in 1968, when thousands of Jews were purged from government jobs and forced to emigrate.

Recent years have witnessed a resurgence of anti-Semitism in Europe. Since 2000, there has been a dramatic increase in attacks on Jewish targets, particularly in France and several other Western European countries. At the same time, there have been new manifestations of anti-Semitism where the target, rather than individual Jews or local Jewish institutions, has been the State of Israel itself. In such cases, where Israel is demonized or its legitimacy as a state is questioned or it is otherwise held to double standards applied to no other country, these manifestations are a form of anti-Semitism. Increasingly, European leaders and institutions have come to recognize this.

In March 2005, the European Union Monitoring Centre for Racism and Xenophobia established a *Working Definition of Antisemitism*, which it distributed to its network of monitors in all twenty-five EU member countries. This definition reads, in part:

Examples of the ways in which antisemitism manifests itself with regard to the State of Israel taking into account the overall context could include:

- Denying the Jewish people their right to self-determination, e.g., by claiming that the existence of a State of Israel is a racist endeavor.
- Applying double standards by requiring of it a behavior not expected or demanded of any other democratic nation.
- Using the symbols and images associated with classic antisemitism (e.g., claims of Jews killing Jesus or blood libel) to characterize Israel or Israelis.
- Drawing comparisons of contemporary Israeli policy to that of the Nazis.
- Holding Jews collectively responsible for actions of the State of Israel.

Israel is a vibrant democracy, and, as such, it is accustomed to vigorous debate and criticism—both from its own citizens and politicians and from outside observers. But, as the EUMC working definition describes, when criticism clearly crosses over to become a venomous, anti-Israel animus, it must be labeled correctly as anti-Semitism.

RABBI ANDREW BAKER is the director of International Jewish Affairs of the American Jewish Committee and a leading expert on anti-Semitism and challenges facing Jewish communities in Europe, particularly Holocaust restitution issues. From 1992-2000, Rabbi Baker served as director of European affairs and was instrumental in developing and implementing programs to promote tolerance in the newly emerging democracies of Central and Eastern Europe.

Judaism
and Jewish Culture

STEVEN BAYME

▶ 43. Where does the Jewish religion come from?

Judaism posed a profound and revolutionary theological transformation. Where paganism assumed a plurality of deities, Judaism flew in the face of contemporary wisdom by assuming a single Deity who had created all of nature.

Judaism constitutes the first of the world's great monotheistic faiths. In that sense, its origins lie in a break from ancient paganism. Ancient men and women looked around themselves and witnessed a plethora of forces of nature significantly affecting their daily lives and over which they could assert no control—fertility, death, climate, the ocean, etc. Behind each of these forces of nature, ancient man posited a deity who presumably might be propitiated and appealed to in times of need. If these forces seemed at times in conflict with one another, they thereby signaled how reality often appeared to be tragic on both individual and collective levels. Thus, questions of why individual women were barren or why natural disasters took place could all be explained as the triumph of particular dark forces at work in the universe.

In this context Judaism posed a profound and revolutionary theological transformation. Where paganism assumed a plurality of deities, Judaism flew in the face of contemporary wisdom by assuming a single Deity who had created all of nature. This monotheistic Creator had brought order out of chaos. Human beings stood at the apex of creation, and they most resembled the Deity through their singular capacity of free will. Much as God had created order in nature, our task as human beings was to create a moral order in society. Lastly, Judaism originated the idea of the Shabbat as the capstone of creation and as a signal to humanity that our six-day work week needs to set aside sacred time for spiritual enrichment via a twenty-four hour retreat from our mundane concerns of productive labor.

This narrative of creation as the original Jewish master story has many implications. First, it categorically rejects any plurality of deities. There is one and only one Creator. Secondly, it hands over to man the task of continuing the work of creation. Because human beings are free, they will be held accountable for the choices they make and the decisions they pursue. Thirdly, the narrative posits a remarkably powerful image of humanity as capable of conquering nature and harnessing it for purposes of societal good. In pronounced contrast to pagan images of humanity as dependent upon the whims of impersonal and vague forces of nature as well as on mysterious powers of magic, Juda-

<—————————————————————————

Previous page: A Torah scroll. Photo by R. Pach/Forum

Jewish girl lights Sabbath candles as her mother looks on. Courtesy of AJC Archives

ism empowered man to work out his or her own destiny. In fact, by banning witchcraft, sorcery, necromancy, and the like, Judaism was not only warring against superstition, but also signaling that only we hold the key to our future history and destiny. Our potential for good is unlimited, but so is our potential for the demonic. Historical events have, all too often, proven the truth of both sides of that assertion. We have demonstrated the incredible power of technology to improve the quality of human life and even prolong it. Conversely, we have repeatedly demonstrated a virtually limitless capacity for man's inhumanity to man.

In short, the work of creation remains incomplete. Natural disasters are understood as continuing challenges to the work of *tikkun olam*" (repairing the cosmos). It is through our actions of *tikkun* or repair and through raising our own families by becoming parents and grandparents that we become partners with God in the process of creation.

Finally, the Jewish master narrative concludes on a note of human failure. Because Judaism did not triumph in the pagan world of the ancient Near East, a special grant was given to the Jews as a people—the Torah—which enjoins the Jews to become a "holy people" whose distinctiveness lies in speaking truth to power and challenging present-day realities even at the cost of great unpopularity. That narrative is the story of Jewish prophecy, which is less about predicting the future than it is about articulating Jewish teaching in a world in which creation remains incomplete, and some chaos remains pervasive.

STEVEN BAYME serves as national director of the Department of Contemporary Jewish Life of the American Jewish Committee. His department deals with Jewish family issues, Jewish education, Israel-Diaspora relations, Jewish identity and continuity, and intra-Jewish relations. He earned a master's degree and doctorate in Jewish history from Columbia University.

Michael Schudrich

▶ 44. What is the meaning of circumcision, wearing a skullcap, and side curls?

According to Jewish belief, Jews were instructed by God to perform circumcision on the eighth day of a baby boy's life. The basis for this practice is found in Genesis 17: 10-14 and 21:4, where God instructs Abraham to do this act to his eight-day-old son, Isaac. The Torah describes this as a sign of the covenant between God and the Jewish people.

According to Jewish belief, Jews were instructed by God to perform circumcision on the eighth day of a baby boy's life. The basis for this practice is found in Genesis 17: 10-14 and 21:4, where God instructs Abraham to do this act to his eight-day-old son, Isaac. The Torah describes this as a sign of the covenant between God and the Jewish people.

Why circumcision? The Torah doesn't state why, but the rabbis have offered several different reasons. One is that a man is born incomplete until we finish his creation through the act of circumcision. A second reason is that circumcision is done in a place that is very private, as a person's deepest relations with God are also very private. A third reason is that the circumcision takes place on the part of the body through which a man can be most like God, i.e., he can create new life. It is on that very part of the body that approaches being God-like (through the creation of new life) that the sign of the covenant should be.

A *kipa* (in Hebrew) or *yarmulke* (in Yiddish) is the head covering that a Jewish male wears in order to show his deep respect and awe for God. Here is a fascinating example of how two religions share the same ideal, but the opposite custom. In Judaism, we cover our heads to show respect for God while in Christianity, one uncovers one's head in church to show respect for God. Various types of head coverings—including a broad-brimmed black hat trimmed in fur or velvet, known as a *shtreimel*, which is worn particularly by Hasidic groups that originated in Poland—typify the many ways different Jewish communities observe this practice.

Payess, or sidelocks, are a Jewish custom based on a biblical injunction that a Jewish male may not cut the corners of his head nor shave his beard with a razor. (However, it is permited to shave using a scissors or an electric shaver.) The basis of this practice is found in the Torah in Leviticus 19:27. A custom arose that it is better not to cut that part of one's hair at all, and so Yemenite, Hasidic, and other Orthodox men came to grow a beard and *payess*. Today, there are mystical reasons given for this custom.

RABBI MICHAEL SCHUDRICH is the chief rabbi of Poland. American-born, he received rabbinical ordination from Yeshiva University. He served as rabbi of the Jewish Community of Japan from 1983-89. He came to Poland in 1992 to work with the Ronald Lauder Foundation there. In 2000 he was appointed the rabbi of Warsaw and Lodz. He has recently become a Polish citizen.

←

Previous page: Israeli soliders praying at the Nozyk Synagogue in Warsaw. KAI

Next page: Orthodox Jewish boys praying in front of the Western Wall, Jerusalem. Courtesy of Israel's Ministry of Tourism

JOHN T. PAWLIKOWSKI

▸ 45. Why don't Jews recognize Jesus Christ as the messiah?

Jewish thought about the messiah is far from monolithic. It has moved in many directions, and hence it is not surprising that most Jews did not recognize the characteristics of the messianic age in the coming of Jesus.

Christians frequently assume that Jesus' being the messiah is a clear-cut reality that every Jewish person in his day should have recognized if they had read their prophetic biblical texts. The actual situation is far more complicated. Jewish thought about the messiah is far from monolithic. It has moved in many directions, and hence it is not surprising that most Jews did not recognize the characteristics of the messianic age in the coming of Jesus.

A study of biblical, medieval, and modern Jewish texts will reveal a great variety of opinions and attitudes concerning the messiah and the messianic age. One strain of messianic thought focused on the restoration of the house of King David and the reemergence of Israel's ancient greatness as a nation. This strain emphasized the rebuilding of the Temple in Jerusalem. A second strain was somewhat more utopian, viewing the messianic era as involving a cataclysmic break with human history. Its coming would be marked by miracles and wonders, and it would involve a final war between Gog and Magog.

Throughout the centuries prior to the coming of Jesus, the pressure of historical events led the Jewish people to accentuate successively different aspects of their messianic hopes. In the period around Jesus' time, the priestly dimension of the messiah dominated over the royal dimension. Some Jews even came to believe in a double messiah—one, the son of Aaron the priest, and the other, a son of Judah from the royal house of David. The notion of a messiah also took on more political tones in this period, especially after the Roman imperial government took control of Palestine from the Hasmonean Jewish rulers. Because the Jewish writers of the time could not speak out openly against their Roman conquerors, they took to criticizing the injustices they were experiencing under Roman domination through use of apocalyptic imagery that appeared on the surface to refer to the end of the world, but, in fact, was meant to criticize the immediate Roman government. Naming the messiah as "Son of Man," a term taken from the biblical book of Daniel, became a favorite way of expressing Jewish hope for the downfall of the Roman occupying authority. In the Jewish community of Jesus' day many definitely associated the coming of the messiah with the political liberation of Israel from Roman imperial rule.

←―――――――――――――――――――――――――――――――――――

Previous page: Photo by L. Filak

Deliberations during the Second Vatican Council (1963-65) which led to the declaration of *Nostra Aetate*. This precedent-shattering statement of the Church's attitude toward non-Christian religions was a breakthrough in the attitude of Catholics toward Judaism. PAP/CAF

For Christians, the term "messiah" was in competition with other titles for Jesus. Once the Christian community became primarily gentile in membership, it became distanced from the discussions of the nature of the messiah going on within Judaism. Rather, Christianity tended to settle on the eschatological dimension of messianism. This sense of the notion of the messiah saw Jesus as the one who had inaugurated through his coming into history the beginning of the end of history.

Jesus' second coming as messiah would complete this process at some future time. In the interim Jesus would function to make the kingdom of God ever more present through healing, the forgiveness of sins, the special concern for the poor and the outcast, and other activities associated with the full reign of God.

Some Christians also picked up on the notion of the messiah as the divine "Logos" or word of God, a concept found in Jewish literature originating in Alexandria, especially from the Jewish writer Philo. Eventually, the Church Fathers transferred this "Logos" notion into philosophical terms that have served as the basis of thinking about Christ in Christian theology over the centuries. The Church Fathers also based their understanding of messianic Christology on what they had read in the Gospel of John. For John, Christ is the Logos incarnate. He is life, light, salvation, and truth. He is the agent of creation, the way, the door to eternity. While such messianic understanding had some roots in Judaism, it went far beyond what most Jews of the period would recognize as authentic messianic understanding.

The above analysis shows the complexity of messianic thinking at the time of Jesus. What Christians eventually came to see in Jesus Christ went far beyond the messianic vision of the general Jewish community of the day. Hence, Christians should not see Jewish rejection of Jesus as messiah as "spiritual blindness." Recent Church documents, particularly the document from the Pontifical Biblical Commission, have begun to acknowledge Jewish messianic understanding as an authentic alternate messianic interpretation. Some scholars in the Jewish-Christian dialogue have even spoken of the Jewish "no" to Jesus as a positive development that could actually enrich Christian understandings of Jesus.

In short, the research connected with the Christian-Jewish dialogue that began with the Vatican Council II's declaration on the Relations between the Church and the Jewish People has shown us that discussion of the differing meanings of the messiah between Jews and Christians can be a positive source of spiritual enrichment for both faith communities, rather than simply of a source of profound division, as had been the case for centuries.

Father John T. Pawlikowski is professor of ethics and director of the Catholic-Jewish Studies Program at the Catholic Theological Union, part of the ecumenical cluster of theological schools at the University of Chicago.

NAOMI HARRIS ROSENBLATT

▶ 46. What is the role of women in Judaism?

The Bible describes Adam and Eve as both created in God's image and thus of equal value and worth in the eyes of God; both are endowed with the gift of free will by the Creator. It was Eve who first questioned the rules in the Garden of Eden, and it was she who chose experience over security, knowledge and wisdom over innocence. With optimism and faith, she leaves the Garden of Eden with her man to start adult life in the real and imperfect world.

Obviously, the woman's role in Judaism has changed over the last 4,000 years. Ancient Hebrew women were legally subordinate to the male heads of their household, first as daughters to their fathers, and then as wives to their husbands. Sons inherited their father's property and, when married, became the heads of their own families. With marriage, a woman joined her husband's family and passed from the authority of her father to that of her husband.

However, Hebrew women throughout the biblical period, and even into modern times, have frequently put themselves on the line and have proven their strength and resilience. They are recorded as having repeatedly questioned, challenged, and assumed positions of power to protect themselves, their families, and their religious beliefs.

To understand the role of women in Judaism, one must begin with the story of the creation of the first woman, Eve. The Bible describes Adam and Eve as both created in God's image and thus of equal value and worth in the eyes of God; both are endowed with the gift of free will by the Creator. It was Eve who first questioned the rules in the Garden of Eden, and it was she who chose experience over security, knowledge and wisdom over innocence. With optimism and faith, she leaves the Garden of Eden with her man to start adult life in the real and imperfect world.

In the biblical chronicles, women are the indispensable link in the development, survival, and continuity of the Covenant that God struck with the founding generation of Abraham and Sarah. They are depicted as "the glue" in many biblical stories, particularly in Genesis and Exodus, where they often use stratagems to preserve the continuity of the family and the Covenant—from Rebekah's disguising Jacob to fool her husband into giving Jacob the blessing instead of Esau, to Miriam and Yochebed's hiding the infant Moses in an ark among the bulrushes of the Nile, thus saving him from being killed by Pharaoh.

In the book of Esther, read on the Jewish holiday of Purim, Queen Esther saves the Jews from assured annihilation. She risks being killed by reporting to the king on his evil henchman, Haman, who is

---

Previous page: Women's section in the Lodz synagogue. A separate section for women, often in the balcony, is a feature of Orthodox synagogues and can be seen in the architecture of synagogues from the Middle Ages.
Courtesy of the City of Lodz Office

Young Jewish woman, Szura Meszerowska, reading a book, Gdansk, 1925.
Courtesy of USHMM

planning to kill all the Jews. Her heroism and intelligence in standing up to the danger are the hallmarks of a young woman, who, despite her limited legal status, struggled to make her voice heard and made a profound difference.

The male head of the family, holding the legal authority, often practiced polygamy in biblical times. Women were sometimes abused, humiliated, and even raped, as recorded in the biblical story of Amnon and Tamar. Monogamy became the norm only during rabbinic times and was extolled by the Talmud; polygamy was forbidden to Ashkenazi Jews by a ruling of Rabbi Gershom ben Yehuda around 1000 C.E., though some Sephardic and Oriental communities continued the practice until modern times, when civil law ended it.

What is intriguing about women in the biblical narrative is how frequently they circumvent male authority, sometimes even subverting it, and yet they are never punished for their insubordination. On the contrary, the biblical text treats the women with deep sympathy, is sensitive to their plight, and records that they are ultimately rewarded for their boldness.

In the Hebrew Bible, sexuality is by no means a secret, sinful, or forbidden subject. Instead, sex is discussed with remarkable openness, with no trace of prudishness. The Song of Songs celebrates in explicit terms the sensual love between Shulamite and her lover (although the rabbinic commentaries reinterpret the text as an allegory of the love between God and Israel). The Bible regards sexuality as the Creator's gift, integral to all human life, to be used as a tool for strengthening the bonds of intimacy, trust, companionship, and responsibility and, of course, generating new life.

In post-biblical times Jewish law redefined the roles of men and women, reflecting contemporary culture and economics. For example, while fundamentally in Jewish marriage the woman is "acquired" by the man, the method of acquisition goes from a biblical "bride price" paid to the father, to a "dowry" given to the newly established home, to the promise of a fixed sum of money to be paid to the woman upon dissolution of the marriage through either divorce or death. The contract that ensures this latter payment is called the *ketuba* and is read at the wedding ceremony. Developed to protect the woman, the *ketuba* describes what the husband is required to provide his wife within the marriage—food, clothing, shelter, and sexual relations.

Rabbinical students at Hebrew Union College, the seminary of the Reform Movement in Judaism. In Reform and Conservative Judaism today women may become rabbis. Photo by Stacey Nolish

Sexual intimacy is one of the expectations between husband and wife. Rabbinic literature is specific about how often a husband, according to his profession, should have sexual relations with his wife. On holidays of celebration, like the Sabbath, it is a double good deed for a married couple to have sexual relations. The goal is to strengthen the bond between the couple, from which the whole family will benefit.

Jewish women were not only given rights, but were expected to fulfill certain roles. The traditional roles gave primacy to women's responsibilities in the home. Thus women were not required to fulfill certain time-bound, out-of-the-house religious responsibilities, such as participating in public prayer services or being a witness in court, that might take them away from home. Other homebound responsibilities were considered peculiarly incumbent upon women, such as lighting the Sabbath or holiday candles or braiding the Sabbath bread. But it is important to understand women's role as extending well beyond these. The traditional roles for women were protected and in many ways preferred, but not mandated; a woman (in most Jewish communities) who wished to participate in public prayer services could do so.

Today in America there are four religious movements in Judaism: Orthodox, Conservative, Reform, and Reconstructionist, representing varying levels of observance and beliefs. The Orthodox, being most observant, keep the laws of *kashrut* (dietary laws), pray three times a day, observe holiday-related laws, such as not driving or operating any electrical equipment on the Sabbath, and are also most strict about gender-defined distinctions. Orthodox women follow a code of modesty that involves wearing skirts or dresses that extend below the knees and sleeves that cover the arms to the elbows or below. They may wear a wig or hat or other head covering so that their husband is the only man to see their hair uncovered.

Reform women do not wear wigs and dress as they please. They express their Jewish identity in many ways, such as Sabbath traditions and transmitting Jewish values and obligations to the next generation. Reform women actively lead and participate in the public prayer services and also read from the Torah. Reform and Reconstructionism were the first branches of Judaism to ordain women as rabbis (which means literally "teacher," but involves public leadership roles).

Conservative Judaism came later to the ordination of women rabbis and to women's participation in public prayer. Today most Conservative synagogues count women as a part of the required quorum for a prayer service and call them to read from the Torah, although the degree of egalitarianism practiced varies from Conservative synagogue to Conservative synagogue.

Conservative, Reform, and Reconstructionist women have a public bat mitzvah ceremony, a rite of passage involving taking on the privileges and obligations of an adult Jew. Orthodox women also become a bat mitzvah, but usually the ceremony is private and does not involve the woman actively leading the prayer service. (Some Modern Orthodox women do lead services and read from the Torah in a women-only prayer group.)

One sacred value held in common by women of all movements in Judaism is Jewish education. A strong emphasis is put on ethics, beliefs, and Jewish history. Lively discussions, interpretations, and questions are encouraged, and women are both teachers and students.

The Jewish woman is held in such high esteem in her family that it is her Jewish identity rather than that of the father that determines the identity of the children. Throughout Jewish history and to the present it has been women who have been the backbone of the family, Jewish continuity, and culture. While legally women were subordinate to the men in their lives, they have tested the limits, questioned what they felt was wrong, and fought for what they thought was right. Women have not been punished for their insubordinate behavior, but instead have been rewarded for their willingness to stare down the threat of danger. As depicted in the Bible again and again, they are bold, courageous, and heroic. For this reason, they are considered "the glue" that binds their families and cultural traditions together.

DR. NAOMI HARRIS ROSENBLATT is a psychotherapist, teacher, and author of *After the Apple. Women in the Bible: Timeless Stories of Love, Lust and Longing* (Miramax Books, 2005) and *Wrestling with Angels: What Genesis Teaches Us About Our Spiritual Identity, Sexuality and Personal Relationships* (Dell, 1995).

DAVID M. GORDIS

▶ 47. Is Jewishness only a religion?

There is no doubt that at the core of the Jewish experience is the Jewish religion, and the insight of ethical monotheism, i.e., the assertion that the world was created and shaped by an ethical God who establishes standards of moral behavior for humankind. It is also true that early in its history the dimension of national existence became central to the Jewish experience, with the establishment of the Jewish nation in the Land of Israel.

The easy way of responding to this question would be to simply say, "No, it is not only a religion." The more difficult challenge is to convey what "Jewishness" is—if, in fact, it is not just a religion. To an extent, the answer is anticipated by the term "Jewishness," the experience of being Jewish, in the question, as distinguished from "Judaism," more clearly representing the religion. But even that distinction does not adequately convey the challenge of finding an accurate way to describe the phenomenon of Judaism.

Sociologists have struggled to place Jews and Judaism into a classical category as a religion, ethnic group, nationality, or culture. None of these classifications proves adequate, because all are part of the phenomenon of "Jewishness," but none describes it satisfactorily.

There is no doubt that at the core of the Jewish experience is the Jewish religion, and the insight of ethical monotheism, i.e., the assertion that the world was created and shaped by an ethical God who establishes standards of moral behavior for humankind. It is also true that early in its history the dimension of national existence became central to the Jewish experience, with the establishment of the Jewish nation in the Land of Israel.

But a complex history transformed Jews into a "world people," perhaps the best capsule descriptor that can be accurately applied. While the ideal of national existence in its homeland was always sustained, Jews developed creative Diaspora communities throughout the many lands of Jewish dispersion. The Jewish community shaped a rich culture that reflected complex interactions with host countries, including a rich and extensive literature and linguistic tradition, embodying creativity not only in the Hebrew language, but also in a set of languages that embodied these interactions, such as Aramaic, Judeo-Arabic, Ladino (Judeo-Spanish), and Yiddish, which developed as a Judeo-German language. The rich literary creativity in these languages embraced both religious and secular subjects, prose and poetry, liturgy and philosophy, reflecting the complexities of the Jewish experience and shaping it.

Previous page: Menorah in front of the Israeli Parliament (Knesset) building. The menorah is both a Jewish religious symbol and the national emblem of Israel. Courtesy of Israel's Ministry of Tourism

Twentieth-century philosopher and theologian Mordecai M. Kaplan contributed a useful concept of how Jews viewed the phenomenon of Jewishness and the way it was viewed by others. His *magnum opus* was entitled *Judaism as a Civilization*. Kaplan sought, with some success, to convey the complexity of the Jewish experience and to suggest that it embraced religion, culture, ethnicity, and nationalism. Kaplan's formulation has been widely accepted by people of quite diverse views as to the fundamental defining nature of Judaism and Jewishness.

This complexity explains a reality that some find difficult to grasp: Despite the unchallenged assertion of the religious core of the Jewish experience, throughout Jewish history individual Jews and groups of Jews have chosen to focus on one or another dimension of Jewishness and to either underemphasize or reject other dimensions. This explains the phenomenon of secular Jews, nationalist Jews, cultural or ethnic Jews. The ability to shape Jewish identity out of the tapestry of Jewish civilization forms part of the ongoing and evolving reality of this unusual and creative "world people."

RABBI DAVID M. GORDIS is president and professor of rabbinics at Hebrew College and founding director of the National Center for Jewish Policy Studies. He also serves as member of the Executive Committee of the American Foundation for Polish-Jewish Studies.

future

Previous page: Participants in the meetings of Polish and Jewish youngsters organized by the Forum for Dialogue Among Nations, April 2006.
Photo by B. Osser

Maciej Kozlowski

▶ 48. Is friendship between Poland and Israel in our shared interest?

In international relations, as in life, it's always better to have friends than enemies. Nations understand this only too well, spending millions to present themselves and their countries in the most favorable light. Doing so results in significant material gains, not in the least politically. When it comes to international conflicts, the friendship of other countries, even geographically distant ones, is invaluable.

Painting by Wilhelm Sasnal, *Poland-Israel.*

In international relations, as in life, it's always better to have friends than enemies. Nations understand this only too well, spending millions to present themselves and their countries in the most favorable light. Doing so results in significant material gains, not in the least politically. When it comes to international conflicts, the friendship of other countries, even geographically distant ones, is invaluable.

Understandably, given our shared history, relations between Poland and Israel could be either very good or very bad, but never indifferent. For a long time after the severing of diplomatic relations in 1967, and especially after the anti-Semitic campaign of 1968, until the renewal of ties in 1989 between then-Communist Poland and Israel, a silent hostility reigned. In practice, that meant negative propaganda and a complete lack of contact. When relations were once again restored, democratic Poland began to change this state of affairs.

Economically, our two countries are almost perfect complements; each produces what the other imports, creating vast opportunities for

←

Previous page: March of the Living in Oswiecim. Photo by A. Chelstowski/Forum

trade. Israel invests capital in Poland because it offers a gateway for influence across the entire European Union. Great opportunities also exist in the realm of tourism. For the ever wealthier and increasingly globe-trotting Poles, the Holy Land, situated in the temperate Mediterranean zone, presents a dream destination. Increasing numbers of Israelis travel to Poland to search for their roots, and are also discovering the charms of our green pastures, lakes, forests, spas, and interesting historical monuments.

From the Israeli point of view, friendly relations with Poland are important for strictly political reasons. Isolated in its geographic region, Israel is engaged in a difficult diplomatic struggle for recognition by its neighbors and is grappling with the plague of terrorism; thus, Israel needs, at minimum, an understanding of its situation, if not international support. Most of all, it needs this support from Europe, with which it is more closely connected historically and culturally than with its great ally across the ocean, the United States. Poland, one of the largest countries in the European Union, a member of NATO and therefore a faithful ally of the U.S., is an exceptionally valuable partner—all the more so because, in Poland, more than in other European countries, there exists an understanding of Israel's challenges.

For Poland, a friendly relationship with Israel is not only repayment of old debts to a nation with whom we are connected by a centuries-long shared history. Poland, like all countries, tries constantly to improve its image in the world. This image is marred through accusations put forward, time and again, of Polish anti-Semitism. Many of these accusations, unfortunately, have their historical justifications. The present day also provides regrettable grounds in this matter.

Yet many of these accusations are baseless, founded on stereotypes and garden-variety ignorance. Attempts to falsify recent history also occur, as, for example, in the widespread use of the expression "Polish concentration camps." Working with Israel to oppose this falsehood is an issue of foremost importance to Poles. And on Poland's domestic front, friendship and a close relationship to Israel are the best medicine for the yet-to-be-cured disease of anti-Semitism.

Above all, there is simply so much that binds Poles and Israelis to each other. It is high time to strengthen these bonds with something tangible, both between our countries and between our peoples.

DR. MACIEJ KOZLOWSKI is a historian, diplomat, former ambassador of the Republic of Poland to Israel, and former Polish deputy minister of foreign affairs.

ROMAN FRISTER

▶ 49. Do Israelis accept the existence of a Palestinian state?

Yes, the majority of Israelis do. But like everything in the shadow of this conflict between two peoples, the politics on both sides are conditional, as is the state that is to become Israel's neighbor.

Yes, the majority of Israelis do. But like everything in the shadow of this conflict between two peoples, the politics on both sides are conditional, as is the state that is to become Israel's neighbor.

Significant opinion polls in Israel have shown a growing acceptance of a two-state solution and support for the existence of a sovereign, democratic, peacefully disposed Palestine as a neighbor to the Jewish state. Positive responses have exceeded 65 percent, but they fall rapidly after every terrorist attack on the Israeli civilian population. During periods of comparative calm, they return to their earlier level. These meanderings of public opinion are, after all, deeply rooted in reality. No one wants Islamic fundamentalists on their doorstep, openly supporting jihad against all religions, cultures, or nations that do not recognize Allah as their Creator.

The victory of the lists fielded by Hamas, perceived worldwide as a terrorist organization, as well as the public announcement by the new prime minister Isma'il Haniya, that he would never acknowledge Israel's right to exist in the Middle East, considerably reduced Israeli willingness to reach a far-reaching compromise.

Within the Palestinian Authority there has been, for years, a battle over the character of a future free Palestine. Armed Islamic organizations, supported by the Iranian ayatollahs, are working toward the creation of a state based on Koranic law; on the other hand, President Mahmoud Abbas (Abu Mazen), a pragmatic leader prone to collaboration with the West, has been seeking understanding with the United States and the European Union. The Polish Republic gave its sign of support for a peaceful, democratic Palestine by opening, for the first time in history, a Polish mission in Ramallah.

Most Israelis want peace. Any reasonably thoughtful person understands that there cannot be peace without a compromise that is basically satisfying to Palestinian national aspirations. But for now, Hamas's victory in the elections plunges any possible settlement of this conflict into an unforeseeable future.

Reaching a compromise will not be easy, not only because the negotiating table is strewn with the corpses of the ongoing conflict, but

---

←

Previous page: Israeli Prime Minister Ariel Sharon and Palestinian Authority President Mahmoud Abbas during a metting, July 1, 2003. epa/PAP

also because each side is pitted against its own opposition. In Israeli society, the strong convictions of some 220,000 Jewish settlers in the West Bank as well as the Orthodox rabbis and political parties who support them cannot dictate political solutions for the Israeli majority. If achieving a truly peaceful resolution to the conflict requires giving up a considerable part of the West Bank, any government that makes that decision will undoubtedly need a majority in parliament or, as some propose, an affirmative vote in a national referendum. But that majority must be convinced there is a partner for peace on the other side.

The evacuation of the Jewish settlements in the Gaza Strip in summer 2005 and the ruling party's plan to dismantle another 70 settlements on the West Bank show which tendencies are dominant. But we should not be deluded. For years, all the efforts to reach a compromise have turned out to be futile: one step forward, two steps backward.

ROMAN FRISTER, born in Poland, is a writer and journalist living in Israel. He is the director of the Koteret School of Journalism and Communication in Tel Aviv, and a correspondent for the Polish weekly *Polityka* (Politics). He is the author of such books as *The Cap: The Price of a Life* and *Impossible Love*.

Leszek Kolakowski

▶ 50. What will relations between Poles and Jews be like in the future?

Twenty years from now there will be no one among us who remembers the Second World War. Nor will there be any Jews who have personal memories of the Holocaust. Historical memory will remain, of course, but it will be ever less laden with living emotion.

Twenty years from now there will be no one among us who remembers the Second World War. Nor will there be any Jews who have personal memories of the Holocaust. Historical memory will remain, of course, but it will be ever less laden with living emotion. This is similar to the way people of my generation retain some emotional residue concerning the issue of World War I, which we know about from the older generation and from school. Does this mean that, as the living memory of those times is extinguished, there will no longer be anti-Semitism in Poland? No, it does not.

The symptoms of anti-Semitism were alive in Poland, and actually increased, during the years leading up to the Second World War, but one would be hard-pressed to name any significant anti-Semitic poets or writers of that time. Among our most eminent artists, many demonstrated friendship vis-à-vis Jews—suffice it to list Adam Mickiewicz, Juliusz Slowacki, and Cyprian Norwid, not to mention the outstanding cultural creators of Jewish origin. Nonetheless, anti-Semitism is a splendid invitation for idiots: They can use it to justify their own frustrations, envy, and intellectual disabilities. (For example, asking, "Whose fault is it?" and answering "the Jewish conspiracy, Jews rule the world," etc). Anti-Semitism, which exists today on the fringes of Polish life, does not direct itself against the few Jews who still go to synagogue and bury their kin in Jewish cemeteries, but rather against mythical Jewish monsters familiar from Nazi tabloids.

Anti-Semitism does not depend on the presence or roles of Jews in society. German Jews were, for the most part, culturally Germanic, and there were fewer of them than Jews in Poland, and yet the bloodiest hatred toward them, nevertheless, developed in Germany.

Anti-Semitism will doubtless linger on the margins of Polish society, with no meaningful influence on daily life. However, our relations with Israel will be less and less tied to Polish history. I am pleased that today there exist Polish-Israeli cultural contacts, that there are young people in Poland who, although they do not have Jewish ancestry, study Jewish history and learn Hebrew and Yiddish. It is important that there be such knowledgeable people, but increasingly (though never entirely) they will resemble specialists in Iberian or Scandina-

←
Previous page: Crowd with flags of Poland and Israel, during the pilgrimage of John Paul II to Poland in 2002. Photo by A. Chelstowski/Forum

258

Participants in the meetings of Polish and Jewish youngsters organized by the
Forum for Dialogue Among Nations, April 2006. Photo by B. Osser

vian culture. One cannot predict to what degree Israeli cultural life will continue to be Jewish life as we knew it from the Jewish shtetls in Poland, which have now disappeared into history. Therefore, it is important that someone preserve the history of Polish Jewry.

PROF. LESZEK KOLAKOWSKI is a prominent Polish philosopher. Until 1968, he lectured at Warsaw University, and thereafter he has lived in exile. Currently he is a fellow of All Saints' College at Oxford. His primary interests are in the history of philosophy, the philosophy of culture, and the philosophy of religion. Aside from philosophical works such as *Conversations with the Devil*, he has written literary works, such as *Main Trends in Marxism*.

The Forum for Dialogue Among Nations is a non-profit Polish organization whose mission is to foster Polish-Jewish dialogue, eradicate anti-Semitism and teach tolerance through education.

The Forum fulfils its mission through seminars, publications, exhibitions, and exchange programs targeted at Polish and Jewish youth and leaders.

Leaders' Dialogue. In collaboration with the American Jewish Committee, the Forum organizes annual leaders exchange programs from both Polish and American Jewish communities.

Youth Dialogue. The Forum organizes meetings of Polish and Jewish youth. The meetings are preceded by workshops about tolerance, conducted in many Polish schools.

Historical Dialogue. We organize exhibitions, publish books, and create educational projects about Jewish history for the Polish public. Our goal is to restore among Poles and Jews the memory of their shared past.

For more information about Forum for Dialogue Among Nations, please visit our website at www.dialog.org.pl

The American Jewish Committee protects the rights and freedoms of Jews the world over; combats bigotry and anti-Semitism and promotes human rights for all; works for the security of Israel and deepened understanding between Americans and Israelis; advocates public policy positions rooted in American democratic values and the perspectives of the Jewish heritage; and enhances the creative vitality of the Jewish people.

Founded in 1906, it is the pioneer human-relations agency in the United States. The American Jewish Committee is a membership organization with eight overseas offices, thirty-two U.S. offices, tweenty-two international partners, including the Union of Polish Jewish Communities, and more than 150,000 members and supporters.

Poland has long been a special interest of AJC, given the tragic history of the Jewish community there, the efforts to support the small community that emerged after World War II, and the continuing work to strengthen understanding and ties among Poland, the American Jewish community, and Israel. With offices in both Jerusalem and Warsaw, AJC plays a central role in furthering this important relationship. AJC sponsors the National Polish American-Jewish American Council and was the first nongovernmental organization to publicly support the inclusion of Poland in the first round of NATO expansion in 1995.

For more information about American Jewish Committee, please visit our website at www.ajc.org

The book was published with financial assistance from

**The Task Force for International Cooperation
on Holocaust Education, Remembrance and Research**

The Task Force for International Cooperation on Holocaust Education, Remembrance and Research consists of representatives of governments and non-governmental organizations. Its purpose is to encourage activities on Holocaust education, remembrance and research in member and other interested countries and to place political and social leaders' support behind the need for Holocaust-related activities both nationally and internationally.

**The Taube Foundation for Jewish Life and Culture
Jewish Heritage Initiative in Poland**

The Jewish Heritage Initiative in Poland, established in 2003, aims to nurture the revival of Jewish life in Poland, further awareness of this resurgence among Jews and non-Jews, and foster positive interest in Poland among American Jews.
This mission reinforces the Taube Foundation's broader purpose of sustaining Jewish culture in the diaspora in the face of assimilation and loss of Jewish identity.